BIRTHTIMES

MICHEL GAUQUELIN

BIRTH-TIMES

A Scientific Investigation of the
Secrets of Astrology

Translated by Sarah Matthews

Hill and Wang · New York

A division of Farrar, Straus & Giroux

© Michel Gauquelin 1983
Translation copyright © 1983 by Basil Blackwell
Publisher Limited
Published in Great Britain as
The Truth About Astrology

Printed in the United States of America

First American edition, 1983

ISBN 0-8090-3083-1

Contents

Preface:
To each his own Truth?

When I come across a book claiming to be the 'truth' about something, my suspicions are aroused. My first reaction is that what I am about to read is primarily the author's own truth for, in science as in other aspects of life, one law or dogma can never be described as the whole truth and nothing but the truth. I would like the reader who has just opened my book, whether friendly or hostile to astrology, to bear this in mind. Everyone who sets out to discover what is true or false about something does so with the spirit of inquiry and intellectual ability available to them, but neither attribute comes to us in equal shares.

Where astrology is concerned, the opposing camps have confronted each other over the centuries, without one side being able to convince the other. Very few scientists nowadays believe in 'the influence of the stars'; it is considered an antiquated hypothesis. Astrologers are generally lumped together with flat-earthers, believers in a geocentric universe and creationists, and regarded as, at best, amiable eccentrics or, at worst, dangerous exploiters of human credulity. As for non-scientists, I suspect the majority have at least a sneaking regard for the pronouncements and predictions of astrologers – much to the indignation of the scientific establishment.

The truth about astrology is certainly not easy to arrive at. It remains an enigma, its origins shrouded in mystery, as the few people who have attempted an impartial investigation of the subject know only too well. I speak from experience about the difficulty of penetrating its secrets. I became deeply interested in astrology as a young man and have devoted more than 30 years' research and critical thought to it. It seemed to me that a set of methods and beliefs which had claimed the attention of the ablest minds over the centuries and still enjoyed widespread popularity among many peoples and cultures was worth investigating, despite (or even because of) my deep scepticism and doubts. What I have discovered has, I confess, led me to modify my opinions. This book will reveal how and why.

Astrology is often described as a fossil science, as mere superstition. Others maintain that it is the cradle of all sciences, the fount of wisdom. But few have tried to prove its claims. Everyone tends to take a stand according to their own intellectual prejudices, becoming more inflexible the more ignorant they are about it. Of course, we all have certain natural inclinations that make us prefer one approach to another, and this applies in any subject, whether political, scientific, religious or artistic. Believing or not believing in astrology is essentially a question of one's point of view – a partiality we should not be afraid to admit.

I was and am by no means immune to intellectual prejudices about astrology; but I have tried, in the course of hundreds of experiments, including the examination of hundreds of thousands of birth dates, to keep my preconceptions in perspective, to stick by my results and to draw the appropriate conclusions from them, however much these might have varied from what I had expected. That is how I have managed – at least, I hope I have managed – to winnow out truth from error and to separate what might be valid laws from wild ideas. During my search for the truth about astrology, I have had both negative and positive results. I describe these in this book and readers will be able to judge for themselves how far my observations support or refute the traditional doctrines of astrology.

My scientific detractors have sometimes dubbed me a 'neo-astrologer' and described my observations as 'neo-astrology' – labels they clearly regard as insulting. For a long time I resented this, but no longer. What do names matter? It is the facts that count, and the methods and the data I have used are as open to confirmation or refutation as in any other field of research. I hope that my 'neo-astrology' will be a tree that bears sound fruit. For that to happen, reality and what I describe as the truth about astrology will have to meet somewhere. Future scholars will be able to judge whether I have done my work well or badly, and whether the fruits of my research have the bitter taste of error or the more palatable flavour of reason.

Prelude:
Astrology Judged

At the end of 1975, 192 'leading scientists' – of whom 19 were Nobel Prize winners and among whom were numbered B. F. Skinner, Fred Hoyle, Konrad Lorentz, Linus Pauling and Sir Francis Crick – signed a manifesto against astrology in the American journal, the *Humanist*. This statement was published on the initiative of the well-known American astronomer, Bart J. Bok, emeritus professor of astronomy at the universities of Harvard and Arizona, and was distributed to the media all over the world. Much more than an indictment, it was intended as the death sentence for astrology, without right of appeal.

Because of the scientific prestige of its signatories and the impact it made, the manifesto is worth looking at in depth. It begins:

Scientists in a variety of fields have become concerned about the increased acceptance of astrology in many parts of the world. We, the undersigned – astronomers, astrophysicists, and scientists in other fields – wish to caution the public against the unquestioning acceptance of the predictions and advice given privately and publicly by astrologers. Those who wish to believe in astrology should realize that there is no scientific foundation for its tenets.

In ancient times people believed in the prediction and advice of astrologers because astrology was part and parcel of their magical world view. They looked upon celestial objects as abodes or omens of the gods and thus intimately connected with events here on earth; they had no concept of the vast distances from the earth to the planets and stars. Now that these distances can and have been calculated, we can see how infinitesimally small are the gravitational and other effects produced by the distant planets and the far more distant stars. It is simply a mistake to imagine that the forces exerted by stars and planets at the moment of birth can in any way shape our futures.

And the statement ends:

Acceptance of astrology pervades modern society. This can only contribute to the growth of irrationalism and obscurantism. We believe that the time has come to challenge directly and force-fully the pretentious claims of astrological charlatans. It should be apparent that those individuals who continue to have faith in astrology do so in spite of the fact that there is no verified scientific basis for their beliefs and, indeed, that there is strong evidence to the contrary.[1]

Such attitudes are not new. When Jean-Baptiste Colbert, minis-ter to Louis XIV, created the Académie des Sciences Française in 1666, he specifically excluded astrology. That was its first 'official' scientific condemnation. Some 300 years later, it has proved necessary to denounce it all over again, with the maximum of publicity. Astrology is clearly a tenacious belief.

Why must it be so humiliated? If nearly 200 'leading scien-tists' take the trouble to attack it publicly, then astrology must surely have an enormous – and enormously unhealthy – influence on our lives and on our thinking. George Abell, one of the signatories of the statement and chairman of the department of astronomy at the University of California, Los Angeles, explains it thus:

In my introductory astronomy classes for the general (non-science) university students, I find that about a third of them profess to believe in astrology. Some of my (non-science) univer-sity faculty colleagues believe in astrology, and my wife and I have a number of personal friends who take it quite seriously. Astrology pretends to be, and to many sounds like, a science. We find a situation wherein a large segment of the population believes in a 'science' that scientists generally reject.

To some, astrology is doubtless a kind of escape. We are expe-riencing today a growing fascination with the occult and mysticism. Perhaps some people are searching for easy answers to hard problems in life, or for a way to avoid the responsibility of making everyday decisions. To others, astrology has become a divine revelation, a pure truth – that is, a genuine religion . . . People today, especially the younger generation, have grown up with television, with sophisticated computers, with astronauts walking on the moon, and with space vehicles successfully exploring the planets . . . To many, these things are miracles that they have taken for granted. In fact, people have become so used to miracles that they are often willing to accept anything, especially when it is presented as fact in the name of science and when the media are full of propaganda on its behalf. Such is surely the case with astrology . . . Astrology has a jargon – trines, conjunctions, transits, progressions, forces, cycles and so forth – that gives it the superficial trappings of a science. How are most people to know the difference?[2]

Whether or not one accepts this analysis, it is true that astrology is spreading, particularly among the young. Surveys in several countries show that astrology is something which large numbers of our contemporaries believe in, to a greater or lesser degree. The historian of astrology, Bouché-Leclercq, must (if his scepticism allows him to) be turning in his grave. In his scholarly work of 1899, *L'Astrologie Grecque*, he claimed: 'It is possible to write the history of astrology now that it is definitively dead.'[3] Yet here it is, up and about again as we approach the year 2000, some 20 years into the space age. The psychiatrist and psychoanalyst, C. G. Jung, was perhaps the first to perceive the discrepancy: 'The cultural Philistines', he wrote, 'believed until recently that astrology had been disposed of long since and was something that could safely be laughed at. But today, rising out of the social deeps, it knocks at the doors of the universities from which it was banished some 300 years ago.'[4] Indeed, it is knocking rather insistently.

It must be admitted there's something paradoxical about the situation, when it's possible for man to walk on the Moon and space probes have landed on Mars and Venus. Increasingly detailed photographs have been taken of Jupiter and Saturn; and what do these photographs show? On the surface, not much – some stones, various gases and clouds and a conspicuous lack of life – nothing, certainly, to suggest that these planets might

have any sort of influence on the lives of men. Why should they
– such small spheres in comparison with the Sun, revolving, like
the Earth itself, around it? In the giant cosmic pinball machine
of our solar system we will look in vain for the 'tilts' which set
off our destinies. Nobody has found any gods behind the planets, as the Chaldeans believed were there, any more than they
have found St Thomas Aquinas' angels pushing them. No one,
in short, has discovered anything positive in favour of astrology.

When some 200 scientists – teachers in the best universities,
Nobel Prize winners – say there is nothing to astrology, they
expect you to believe them. One supposes that, as true scientists,
they did not make their declaration lightly. One assumes that
they have studied the subject and that their declaration is backed
by a solid body of proof. After all, the manifesto concludes: 'It
has been proved that astrology has no scientific base and that
there are well-established proofs of its non-existence.'

So it is worth giving some attention to the article which followed this famous anti-astrological declaration, written by its
instigator, the astronomer Bart J. Bok. In its ten closely printed
pages, one looks in vain for the proofs announced in the manifesto. Indeed, it appears that Professor Bok has never studied
the question: 'At one time', he admits, 'I thought seriously of
becoming personally involved in statistical tests of astrological
predictions, but I abandoned this plan as a waste of time, unless
someone could first show me that there was some sort of physical foundation for astrology.'[5] Returning to the manifesto itself,
we find the much-vaunted proofs against astrology simply are
not there. It turns out to be a peremptory declaration, an out-of-
hand condemnation, based solely on the principle but not the
practice of scientific authority. At the very least, this is a contra-
vention of the old Cartesian maxim that 'nothing should be
taken to be true, or false, that one does not know to be so.' Can a
mere assertion properly be described as intellectually honest?

Some scientists, however, did refuse to sign the anti-
astrological manifesto. Carl Sagan, for instance, professor at the
Center of Radiophysics at Cornell University, is well-known for
his television series *Cosmos* and for his book *Cosmic Connection*,
which speculates on the possibility of contact between our civi-
lization and extra-terrestrial civilizations. In a letter to the editor
of the *Humanist*, he explained the grounds for his refusal:

I find myself unable to endorse the 'Objections to Astrology' statement, not because I feel that astrology has any validity whatever, but because I felt and still feel that the tone of the statement is authoritarian. The fundamental point is not that the origins of astrology are shrouded in superstition. This is true as well for chemistry, medicine and astronomy, to mention only three. To discuss the psychological motivation of those who believe in astrology seems to me quite peripheral to the issue of its validity. That we can think of no mechanism for astrology is relevant but unconvincing. No mechanism was known, for example, for continental drift when it was proposed by Wegener. Nevertheless, we see that Wegener was right, and those who objected on the grounds of unavailable mechanism were wrong. Statements contradicting borderline, folk or pseudo-science, that appear to have an authoritarian tone, can do more damage than good. They never convince those who are flirting with pseudo-science, but merely seem to confirm their impression that scientists are rigid and closed-minded.[6]

Some sociologists and historians of science became involved in the question, too. In an examination of the manifesto, Ron Westrum, a sociologist at Eastern Michigan University, recalled that this was not the first time in the history of science that a declaration based on the principle of authority had been published by a group of scientists against a controversial theory.[7] He then goes on to pose these questions: are the signatories of the condemnation really experts, in the juridical sense of the term, and what would happen in a real trial if the counsel for the defence subjected these witnesses to the rigours of cross-examination? 'Ideally', he writes, 'expertise would come naturally from researchers active in the study of astrology through scientific experimentation, clinical observation, and statistical analysis.' But he continues, 'It is not clear how many of the 192 signers of the protocol have either of these types of expertise. The eminence of these men and women does not allow us to dismiss their opinions lightly, even if they have not familiarized themselves with the relevant literature. Yet we can question whether they have the right to state that "there is no scientific foundation for (astrological) tenets" without having done the necessary homework.' Westrum adds that it is certainly incorrect to assert that, because one is an astronomer, one is necessarily an expert in astrology; he points out that the absence of a 'cross-examination' after the indictment could only encourage a lack of scientific rigour among the signatories, assured as they were of intellectual impunity.

Westrum concludes by recommending that the scientists proceed with caution and reminds them of the case of the meteorites. In 1772 the Académie des Sciences, under the celebrated Lavoisier, the father of modern chemistry, gave its verdict against meteorites: 'These rocks cannot have fallen from the sky, because there are no rocks in the sky.' Thirty-one years later in 1803, the scientific community accepted the existence of meteorites, mainly as a result of the work of Jean Baptiste Biot (1774–1862). As Biot noted in his article on meteorites, judgement should never precede observation: 'It is always the case, when there is a controversial question, that the ignorant believe naively and the semi-schooled come to a decision; but one who has any real understanding examines the facts, because he does not have the temerity to set limits on the capacity of nature.'[8]

Paul Feyerabend, professor at the University of California in Berkeley and the author of *Against Method*, advocates the need for a scientific thinking freed from suffocating dogma. He too has criticized anti-astrological judgements based solely on the principle of authority. While he refuses to defend astrology *per se* and particularly 'as it is practised nowadays by the majority of astrologers', he has nevertheless written about the manifesto that 'the judgement of the "192 leading scientists" rests on an antediluvian anthropology, on ignorance of more recent results in their own fields (astronomy, biology, and the connection between the two) as well as on a failure to perceive the implications of the results they do know. It shows the extent to which scientists are prepared to assert their authority even in areas in which they have no knowledge whatsoever.'[9] The behaviour of the signatories to the 'Objections to Astrology' seems to have confirmed Feyerabend's view, that science is much closer to myth than scientific philosophy would readily allow. Science, he argues, is one of the many modes of thinking developed by man, but not necessarily the best. And what is certain is that science is tactless, noisy and arrogant.[10]

These opinions show that it is possible, at any rate, to question the official orthodoxy. That said, it has to be admitted that condemnation of astrology has been more or less universal among scientists, in Europe as much as in the United States. In France, the venerable Union Rationaliste, inveighing against all 'false sciences', has not spared astrology, although the members of this association have not attempted to demonstrate its lack of validity by carrying out experiments or by monitoring those put to them by researchers. At a meeting of the International Astronomical Union held in Grenoble at the end of 1976, the French-speaking astronomers, aping their American colleagues, circulated an anti-astrological petition based on the transatlantic model.

Astrology is often dismissed by scientists as 'absurd'; it is 'absurd', so it cannot be true. Paul Couderc, astronomer at the Paris Observatory, is a long-standing adversary of astral influence. He concludes a chapter of his book, *L'Astrologie*: 'Scientific astrology has not got a single positive fact to its credit, any more than commercial astrology has. It may be a pity, but it is so.' First published in 1951, the revised edition of 1978 shows that he has not changed his mind (see chapter 5 for further discussion of Couderc's views).[11]

Younger and more influential – at least at the moment – is Jean Claude Pecker, professor of astrophysics at the Collège de France and member of the Académie des Sciences, who has for years been a passionate opponent of astrology. Pecker's style echoes that of the American manifesto. For him, 'the astrological sky is inflexible . . . Astrology establishes between the beings in the heavens and on the earth a dictatorial correspondence. On top of that, it sees a correspondence between the spirits of the living and of the dead. Occasionally, the two aspects of these correspondences get mixed together in curious lucubrations.'[12] A little further on, he laments the fact that 'the amount spent on astrology in the world is noticeably greater than that spent in observatories.' Yet he provides no figures to back up this assertion, which remains open to question when you think how much a radio-telescope costs these days, not to mention the amount expended on space exploration. 'Despite the interdictions of the law and of the church', he states, 'the charlatans proliferate, and women's magazines peddle their futures in a way that has not got anything to do any more with the astrological forays of the Sumerians.'

Against this, one can set the words of Johannes Kepler (1571–1630), writing nearly 400 years ago:

> No man should hold it to be incredible that out of the astrologers' foolishness and blasphemies some useful and sacred knowledge may come, that out of the unclean slime may come a little snail or mussel or oyster or eel, all useful nourishments; that out of a big heap of lowly worms may come a silk worm and lastly that in the evil-smelling dung a busy hen may find a decent corn, nay, a pearl or a golden corn if she but searches and scratches long enough.[13]

A belief that there could be an element of truth in astrology did not stop Kepler from discovering the laws about the movements of the planets which bear his name – one of the most remarkable achievements of the human mind. Indeed, Gérard Simon has shown that it was to a great extent *because* he thought astrology was possible that Kepler was able to carry through his discoveries successfully.[14]

But is it, in any case, really honest to reduce astrology to nothing but the practice of the charlatans of sun-sign astrology? We must not confuse commercial astrology and cosmic influence. In a letter to his friend, Raulin, on 4 April 1871, Louis Pasteur wrote:

> You know I believe in an asymmetric cosmic influence which governs, naturally and constantly, the molecular organization of the immediate essential principles of life, and that in consequence the species of different kingdoms of life are, in their structure, their form, and the disposition of their tissues, in relation with the movements of the universe.

This should be set against the scepticism of the astronomers. Pasteur, after all, still carries as much scientific weight as Professor Bok and Professor Pecker. In this context (and in that of Pasteur's own life and of his own difficulties in convincing his colleagues about the nature of bacterial life-forms), it is worth quoting Marcello Truzzi, head of the department of sociology at Eastern Michigan University:

> To most modern scientists, the idea of significant cosmic influence upon human behaviour seems implausible. The matter is

made worse when no concrete mechanisms are suggested by which such effects are obtained, and made worse still when the explanations offered are couched in language reminiscent of supernaturalism and occultism. Those concerned about the absence of mechanisms seem to overlook similar opposition to Newton's theory of gravity, with its action at a distance, once seen by critics as occult; and some have suggested that Newton may have been untroubled by the action-at-a-distance problem, largely because of his own involvement with astrology.[15]

The sceptical reader will object, quite rightly, that astrologers' assertions are usually improbable, to a degree which is very hard to accept, and that the charlatan air of newspaper horoscopes is particularly worrying in an age where everyone has access to learning. Scientists who have been irritated by the trade in horoscopes can be forgiven for not having gone deeply enough into the question. Besides, it is not up to them to provide proof of the reality of astral influence: it is up to the astrologers themselves. Just because some lunatic declares himself to be a new Christ, it does not mean that you have to mount a campaign to prove he is not a new messiah. It is the same with the claims made by astrologers.

One of the most respected logicians among contemporary scientists is Karl Popper, an Austrian by birth who lives in England. In his authoritative work, *The Logic of Scientific Discovery*, he puts forward the concept of 'falsifiability', perhaps his most significant contribution to scientific logic.[16] 'Falsifiability' is the property of a theory capable of being proved or disproved by the facts. According to Henry Parkinson, 'Popper's notion of falsifiability is surprisingly fruitful. Falsifiability not only allows us to demarcate science from non-science and to weed out worthwhile theories from false ones, it also explains how scientific knowledge grows. Falsification, Popper argues, is the key to the growth of science.'[17]

In short, anything verifiable is 'falsifiable', and anything verifiable has the right to be called 'scientific'.[18] An assertion which cannot be subjected to scientific examination is *a priori* valueless. If I claim that I am the new messiah, it cannot be a scientific assertion because it is not 'falsifiable': it is impossible to prove either that I am right or that I am wrong. An example of a

verifiable theory, on the other hand, is Einstein's theory of rela-
tivity. In fact, this theory is constructed in such a way that
observation could either prove or disprove it. Popper empha-
sizes the point: it is not because observation eventually confirmed Einstein's theory that it is a 'scientific' theory, it is
because of the fact that it could have been seen to be *false*.

And astrology? Popper mentions it in his book and rejects it
as a science, just as elsewhere he dismisses psychoanalysis and
Marxism. He finds that astrological claims are not formulated in
appropriate terms. Believing that to be born with the Sun in
Aries will make for a more daring character than to be born with
the Sun in Cancer cannot, according to Popper, be scientifically
true because it cannot be verified, any more than the Freudian
notion of the unconscious, or Marxist dialectic, or my claiming
to be the new Christ can be verified.

Leaving aside the case against psychoanalysis and Marxism
(antagonistic doctrines made into curious bedfellows by the logic
of Popper's thinking), let us look into the validity of his argument against astrology. Cast in rather less sophisticated terms
than Popper's – though terms which have stood the test of time
– the existence of astrology can be seen as depending on the
answer to two questions:

1 Is it possible to verify the so-called laws of astrology?
2 If so, are they true?

Where the first question is concerned, Popper seems to be
superficially right and fundamentally wrong. He is right
because, however venerable the astrological idea might be, there
is no denying that in the distant past its very essence was allied
to magic, which is not compatible with modern scientific thinking. The signs of the zodiac have a very long history, with a
symbolism going back at least 4,000 years. For instance, the
Chaldeans gave the name of Scorpio to a particular constellation
in which the stars more or less made up the form of a scorpion,
some shaping the pincers and others the poisonous tail of the
creature. By analogy, they attributed to this constellation an
influence consonant with the behaviour of the animal. They
projected the earthly scorpion into the sky, and that, in its turn,
was supposed to have an influence on those born under that
constellation. This kind of astrological inversion still goes on

today. Modern textbooks state that when the Sun moves into
Scorpio at the time of birth, it confers on the newborn child
some of the characteristics of the scorpion – a dangerous,
aggressive and courageous insect, with a fearsome sting, which
sometimes finds self-destruction or suicide the only way out.
The scorpion's aggressiveness can be turned against itself, hence
the tormented, twisted attitude of the astrological sign. Luigi
Aurigemma, in his study of the zodiac sign of Scorpio, has given
a clear account of the symbolic development of the sign from
antiquity to the Renaissance.[19] As far as this symbolism is concerned, contemporary astrologers have changed nothing.

Popper and the anti-astrologists are equally right to protest
against the charlatans of horoscopy. Most people today are
aware of the significance of heredity and environment in shaping
the personality and destiny of the individual. So how can we
possibly accept that our characters, our periods of good or bad
luck, should be rigorously determined by the planets at birth?
Horoscopes, for some astrologers, explain everything and, even
for the most cautious among them, reveal a good deal of our
destiny. Such pretensions are the less acceptable in that the
modern horoscope is, to all intents and purposes, precisely the
same as it was 2,000 years ago at the time of Greek astrology. If
astrology were a science worthy of the name, it would have
evolved over the centuries, like physics since Aristotle, medicine
since Hippocrates, or astronomy since Ptolemy. It has not done
so. That is, perhaps, the most shocking thing about it. Why has
astrology fossilized? Because it is a sort of revealed religion, or
just fantasies and fables for fooling the gullible? Either way,
Popper was right to exclude astrology from the scientific family.

Or else, could it be that astrology – through some unhappy
quirk of fate, through some opportunity overlooked by the
researchers, for some reason or other – has missed out on the
attention necessary for it to be radically transformed over the
years (like physics, astronomy or medicine), in order for it to
become, with progress, the science of the influence of the stars
on men? The disturbing question posed by Kepler, 'Is there a
corn of gold in astrological beliefs?', has remained unanswered.
But if that gold does exist, is it possible to extract it from all the
dross around it? It seems at least, with all due deference to
Popper and the modern astronomers, an attempt worth making.

Because of its very rigidity and its long-fossilized dogmas, handed down in oral and written tradition by people with no critical sense at all, astrology is a doctrine which presents a body of 'laws', a body which is fundamentally coherent, however incoherent it appears on the surface. And these laws, however 'absurd', are usually – though not always – 'falsifiable'.

The influences associated with the 12 signs of the Zodiac or attributed to the Sun, the Moon and the planets can be looked at in this way. For example, if you were born between 21 March and 20 April, you are an Aries. The books on astrology almost all provide the same interpretation of your being an Aries: it means you are 'spontaneous, passionate, combative, given to excitement, enthusiasm, full of initiative, enterprise, delighting in conquest, novelty, and adventure'. We have quoted one astrologer. Experience has shown that another will give almost exactly the same account. That this should appear 'absurd' is fair enough, but I can't accept any claim that 'this absurdity cannot be tested scientifically.'

In short, astrology seems to consist of a whole collection of 'absurdities' which can be studied scientifically. But, to carry out such a study properly calls for a good deal of intellectual courage, since it means running up against the opposition of two orthodoxies, both of them ready to defend their positions tooth and nail: these are traditional astrology and what, according to Thomas S. Kuhn's definition, can be classed as 'normal' science.[20] The compensation, perhaps, is that, at the end of a long road, one is no longer swaddled in comfortable illusions either for or against astrology, and that one knows for sure whether there really is a 'corn of gold' in the midst of all the nonsense of horoscopes and the rest.

But courage is not always enough. Are the means also available to make such a project possible? First of all, we need to see whether there is some sort of *physical* proof that could be applied. The astronomer Bart J. Bok writes:

It seems inconceivable that Mars and the Moon could produce mysterious waves, or vibrations, that could affect our personalities in completely different ways. It does not make sense to suppose that the various planets and the Moon, all with rather similar physical properties, could manage to affect human affairs in totally dissimilar fashions . . . Why should the precise moment of birth be the critical instant in a person's life? Is the instant of conception not basically a more drastic event than the precise moment when the umbilical cord is severed?[21]

Professor Bok does modify his objections with some such phrase as 'in the current state of our knowledge and technological development' and, given that reservation, what he says is true. Nobody could apply a *physical* or palpably measurable proof of the role played by planets or constellations at birth in the destiny of a newborn child.

However, the absence of irrefutable physical proof should not be confused with the non-existence of the phenomenon. The laws of gravity have been accepted ever since Newton, although we are only just beginning to record, by devious routes, the existence of gravitational waves which would explain both Newton's and Einstein's laws.[22] Yet, as far as gravity is concerned, what was needed was being able to 'see' how it worked: its reality was never in doubt.

More often, it is the physical proof of the phenomenon which is required in order to make its existence credible. That is where Galileo ran into difficulties, when he asserted that the Earth revolved round the Sun and that it was not fixed at the centre of the universe. His opponents had an easy time and cannot be blamed, after all, for retorting, 'Prove it!' Galileo could not. Taking a star as a reference point, he would have had to demonstrate that the Earth had changed position during the year in the course of its hypothetical rotation round the Sun, and that the reference star could not therefore be observed in the same place in the sky in the winter as it was in the summer. This is now called stellar parallax. But because his telescope was far too crude, and because the stars are a good deal further away from our solar system than was then thought, Galileo could not prove the existence of the stellar parallax, which would have constituted visible and irrefutable proof of the Earth's rotation round the Sun. Indeed, as all the stars observed appeared to be fixed, there was a strong presumption against Galileo's hypothesis, and he was condemned to disavow his theory by the Inquisition. 'Eppur', si muove!' – and yet it does move, he is supposed to have exclaimed. The reality of stellar parallax was not demonstrated until three centuries later, because its annual value is extremely small: even for the star closest to us, Proxima Centauri, its value is only 0·76 seconds of arc.

And yet, astrology is true, exclaim the astrologers in their turn, even though one can neither see nor record the influence of the planets. So, what can be done? There are, in fact, two ways of verifying astrology – clinical control and statistical verification. The first method consists in assessing the accuracy of astrological predictions and interpretations or, to put it crudely, finding out whether they work or not. It is possible to assess the diagnostic capacity of a doctor or a psychologist in the same way. One might object that failure would call into question the skills of particular astrologers, but that it would not necessarily provide an empirical refutation of astrology as a doctrine. The fact that doctors and psychologists make mistakes in their diagnoses does not prove that medicine and psychology are not true sciences (and what if the experiment had been conducted in Pepys's time?). So, testing the ability of astrologers is an interesting undertaking and one whose results we will examine, although not a decisive answer.

There is a second method – an indirect, but also a more objective and rigorous one – of assessing the value of astrological doctrine as a whole, rather than the ability of some particular practitioner: this is by means of statistics. A statistical law is a natural law like any other, a typical example being the one discovered by Mendel, the father of the science of genetics. 'Having fertilized a sweet-pea flower with smooth-skinned peas with pollen from another flower which gave wrinkle-skinned peas, Mendel observed that the peas from the resulting hybrid were uniformly smooth-skinned. Sowing these peas, and allowing the resulting plants to fertilize each other, he observed that *three quarters* of the new generation had smooth-skinned peas, while the remaining *quarter* had wrinkle-skinned peas.'[23]

After carrying out the experiment a number of times, Mendel always found the same percentages – 75 per cent smooth-skinned peas to 25 per cent wrinkle-skinned peas. He concluded that, genetically, the fact that a pea has a smooth skin is a 'dominant' factor, while a wrinkled skin is a 'recessive' factor. There is no point here going into the role played by this statistical law in the history of genetics. What is significant is to understand that, in isolating the specific characteristic of a plant (whether smooth or wrinkled in this case), Mendel was able to demonstrate a fundamental natural property. And yet – and it is relevant to our present analysis to mention the fact – Mendel's discovery was 'forgotten' for over 50 years, because he had everything against him: he was an amateur – a monk and not a botanist; his law ran counter to contemporary received ideas; and it was statistical and therefore not palpable. This is how Asimov tells the story of Mendel's vicissitudes:

> Mendel . . . conscious of his own status as an unknown amateur, felt it would be wise to obtain the interest and sponsorship of some well-known botanist. In the early 1860s, therefore, he sent his paper to Nägeli, who was the nearest of the prominent botanists of the time. Nägeli glanced through the paper but apparently was repelled by the mathematics. He himself was a biologist of the old school and indulged in rather windy and obscure theorizations. A paper by an unknown monk with no theories but with only painstaking countings and ratios seemed worthless to him. He returned it with brief and cold comments, and this effectively chilled Mendel. To be sure, Nägeli offered to grow some of Mendel's seeds, but he never did and the offer was probably not meant seriously. He did not answer Mendel's later letters, and when Nägeli wrote his major work on evolution twenty years later, he did not mention Mendel . . . Mendel died in 1884, lonely and saddened, never suspecting that he would be famous. Nägeli died in 1891, never dreaming what a terrible mistake he had made.[24]

It was only in 1900 that Hugo De Vries made Mendel's work known to the scientific community. Mendel's 'laws', although entirely statistical, are now officially recognized by science; and since the discovery, in 1962, of the structure of DNA by Watson and Crick, which won them the Nobel Prize, it is now becoming possible to explain these 'laws'. It has taken more than 100 years.

This digression on Mendel has brought us back directly to our subject. It is possible to study the principal rules of astrology statistically. If one could, for instance, demonstrate that children born when Mars was dominant in their horoscopes had a greater chance of succeeding in military professions than children born under other planets, that would confirm the validity of astrology; and if it were possible to estimate, even very roughly, the percentage of military success to be achieved by these little newborn 'Martians', then one would be in a comparable position to Mendel after his scrupulous enumeration of 75 per cent smooth-skinned peas to 25 per cent wrinkle-skinned peas. It would be an uncomfortable position because one would, like him, run up against the views of professional astronomers and biologists, to whom any coherent explanatory theory would have to be proposed. Nevertheless, an astrological law, demonstrated statistically, would be proof that nature at least accepts that law. Even if we had not yet discovered its physical cause, the result could alter our scientific vision of the world.

Part One

In Search of Planetary Effects at Birth

I

The Planets of Success

Is life made up of a succession of haphazard events, or is there a more or less unconscious thread running through and directing our efforts to some sort of specific aim? At the age of 20, I was wildly enthusiastic about everything to do with astrology, although I was almost equally mad about painting and tennis. I wanted to do research into astrology, but had neither the money, nor the time (I was finishing my studies), nor the application necessary. I did, however, have a foggy idea of what was involved. I would go down to the library, between a drawing session in a Montparnasse attic and a tennis match, and copy out the names and dates of birth of people who had made a sufficient mark in life to feature in a dictionary of the famous. When I started, I did not exercise any sort of discrimination, but wrote them down in alphabetical order as they cropped up – artists, scientists, politicians, military leaders and so on. Of course, these lists were only a stage in my thinking; my imagination covered a lot of ground, although I actually achieved very little. The second stage was to write to the offices where these births were registered, in order to find out the hour of birth – an essential piece of information in any serious study of astrology.

More than 30 years later, I can still recall my delight when, after a few inept and fruitless attempts, I received my very first extract from a birth certificate stating the hour of birth. It was February 1949 and the certificate was that of Louis Braille, the inventor of the reading system for the blind which bears his name. Heaven knows why I asked for Braille's hour of birth:

although famous, he hardly belonged to a particularly well-defined professional category – in fact, I have never since been able to make use of him in my statistical researches. That shows the lack of method in my early research. But the enthusiasm remained and, after a year or two of working like this, I had listed a few hundred cases, scattered haphazardly through a wide range of professions.

At the same time, I had already set up some real statistics about the thousands of cases without an hour of birth, in an attempt to verify some of the rules of traditional astrology, including the influence of the signs of the zodiac or particular planetary aspects. The results were less than encouraging and I should, in all logic, have abandoned the whole enterprise then.[1] But I decided to continue and to concentrate on increasing my collection of famous figures with their hours of birth.

It was a very long-term, expensive and obstacle-strewn project, and for that reason I was led, almost despite myself, to observe a certain method – to centre my researches on the outstanding figures in one single profession, rather than flying about like a demented bee from one profession to another, without obtaining a sufficiently large and homogeneous group of cases.

Then the breakthrough came when a close friend, who was very interested in my projects of astrological analysis, showed me a work called the *Index des Membres, Correspondants et Associés de l'Académie de Médecine*.[2] In spite of its rather off-putting title, I found it more enthralling than the most gripping of novels the moment I opened it. Arranged in alphabetical order, the book contained the name, place and date of birth of every French doctor elected to this learned academy since its foundation in 1820 up until 1939.

I decided to make a systematic list of all the names and to write to the register offices of the birthplaces to find out the hour of birth of the greatest possible number of doctors. Even this took me some time, as my financial resources were still limited. In 1951, in spite of everything, I reached the end of the project. I had a list of 576 French doctors, all elected to the Académie de Médecine, with whose help I would be able to extend my statistical researches, which had so far been limited to horoscopes without a birth hour.

The specific hour of birth is of crucial significance. It is this which fixes the position of the planets in their daily movement, what astrologers call their position in the 'houses'. Now scientific research is a narrow gate and nature is not without her caprices. How much simpler it would be if positive planetary effects could be observed without needing to know more than the day and place of birth. After all, astrologers can already construct the entire outline of a horoscope without knowing the birth hour, by calculating the positions of the planets in the signs of the zodiac. It would have been easier still if I had not discovered any sort of planetary effect at all, even with the additional data of the hours of birth (in which case I would not have written this book). But the 576 members of the Académie de Médecine were to prove that nature had more than one trick up her sleeve. Having (painfully) worked out by hand the position of the planets at the hour of birth of each doctor, I made a statistical compilation of my findings. Suddenly, I was presented with an extraordinary fact. My doctors were not born under the same skies as the common run of humanity. They had chosen to come into the world much more often during roughly the two hours following the rise and culmination of two planets, Mars and Saturn. Moreover, they tended to 'avoid' being born following the rise and culmination of the planet Jupiter.

After such a long and fruitless search, here I was, confronted with not one but three astonishing results – all from observing the daily movement of the planets.

Astronomers call this daily movement of the planets their 'diurnal movement', which sounds slightly odd, as though it stopped at night, which of course it doesn't. In order to visualize this movement, you have to remember that the Earth revolves on its axis every 24 hours, causing the succession of days and nights. Every morning, the Sun rises in the East, climbs up in the sky until it reaches its maximum height, at mid-day, and goes down again to set in the West. Then night falls. Invisibly, 'under the Earth', the Sun proceeds on its way to reach its furthest point at midnight, and then follows its curve so that it rises again the next day at more or less the same time as the day before. This movement of the Sun is an apparent movement. If the Earth did not rotate, the Sun would seem to remain fixed in the sky: it would always be day on one side of the Earth, and always night on the other. Of course, the Sun's timetable depends on where you are on the Earth's surface. The Sun rises earlier in London than it does in New York, causing the well-known time-difference between the two. It is a timetable which also depends on the seasons: in the Northern hemisphere, the days are longer in summer because the Sun rises earlier and sets later, while the opposite is the case in the Southern hemisphere. Everyone is familiar with the diurnal movement of the Sun since its effects – its light and its heat – regulate our rhythms of waking and sleeping.

But what about the other heavenly bodies, the Moon and the planets in particular? Naturally, they share in this same apparent diurnal movement. Every day, the Moon and the planets rise, culminate and set just like the Sun, but each at its own time. There are lunar, Venusian, Martian days and so on, just as there are solar days. The Moon and the planets always follow the same path, according to their own, different, timetables. As for the Sun, the same terms of rising and setting are employed, except that the equivalents of midday and midnight are known as 'superior culmination' and 'inferior culmination'. Thus, in the example in figure 1, the 'midday' of Mars – its superior culmination – occurs at 4.35 p.m., and its 'midnight' – its inferior culmination – at 4.35 a.m.

In order to calculate probabilities from the positions of a planet, the circle of its daily movement has to be divided into a number of sectors – 12, 18, 36, etc. These divisions differ as to the details they can reveal, but are equivalent in terms of method.[3] In this way, the Martian day for the 3 October 1952 at Paris can be divided into 12 sectors or celestial sections, as shown in figure 2. It is logical to begin numbering these sectors from when the planet rises and to continue in the direction of its diurnal movement. Supposing you were born on 3 October 1952 in Paris, you can see immediately that, according to the hour of your birth, Mars would be in one sector or another of the circle. At one o'clock in the afternoon, Mars has just risen and is in sector 1; but if you were born at 5 in the afternoon, Mars is in sector 4, following its superior culmination.

I hope the reader will now have a clear idea of diurnal move-

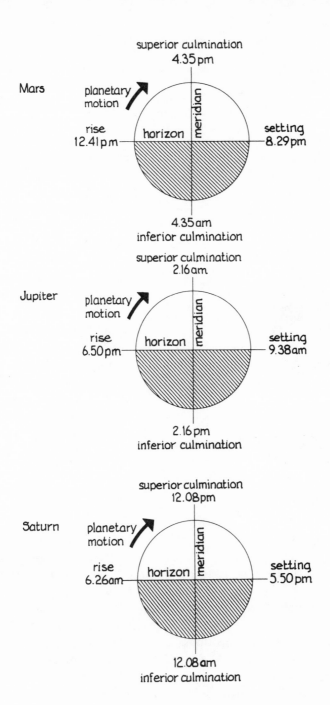

Figure 1   Timetable of the days of Mars, Jupiter and Saturn, on 3
October 1952 in Paris

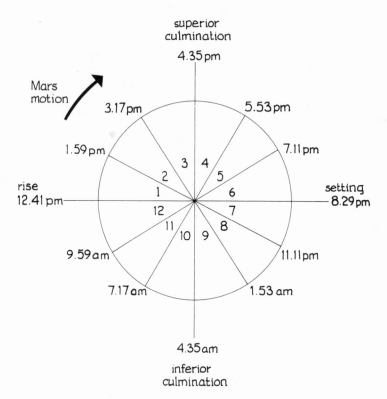

Figure 2 Division into 12 sectors of the day of the planet Mars, on 3 October 1952 in Paris

ment, and of the significance of the hour of birth for situating a planet precisely in one of the sectors of the sky. At the moment of your birth, each body in the solar system is housed in one of the sectors of the celestial wheel – you can picture it as a daily celestial roulette wheel, if you like. But one swallow does not make a summer, and one birth, even yours, does not make a statistic. You need a group of at least several hundred births, before you can add up the number of appearances of, say, the planet Mars in sectors 1, 2, 3, etc., right up to 12.

All this explains why, to realize my ambitious projects, I had to assemble the hour, date and place of birth of hundreds of people in an attempt to find out whether anything abnormal was going on. 'Abnormal' in this case meant an indication that the way the planets were distributed in the different sectors at birth was more than a matter of chance, and that chance had been 'disturbed' by some outside influence.

My medical academicians were born more often than chance would allow after the rise and culmination of the planets Mars and Saturn. Was that proof of a correlation between success as a doctor and the presence of those planets in those sectors of the sky? In spite of wanting to reply in the affirmative, I knew that I had first to find the answer to another question. It was possible that this greater frequency of Mars and Saturn had some simple astronomical or demographic origin. The two planets might have been more likely to be on the rise or at their culmination, rather than at other points in the sky, at the birth of *every* child and not just at the birth of those who later became outstanding physicians. In other words, I had to have as a control a large number of births of people who did not grow up to be outstanding physicians.

These non-doctors had to be born during the same years as the doctors for them to be a viable control group. I managed to get access to the birth registers, on the basis of which I built up my control group, making a systematic list of all the hours of birth recorded on the certificates over a period of several score years. Then I calculated the positions of Mars, Jupiter and Saturn which corresponded to each of these 'ordinary' births. This time, the distribution between the different sectors of these three planets showed nothing abnormal. It was only outstanding doctors who 'chose' to come into the world under Mars and Saturn and to 'avoid' Jupiter.

Still, I had to be careful not to deceive myself. The results I had obtained, although very clear, could still have been a chance combination. I had to bear in mind that this experiment was not my first attempt at establishing a relation between the planets and mankind. One day, I was bound to come across a result which was out of the ordinary. If you chance your arm on a lottery ticket every week, sooner or later you will win a prize, usually a fairly small one. I had won the jackpot, in fact, but while the odds against one individual winning the jackpot are extremely high, nevertheless somebody has to win it every time.

To make sure that I really had encountered a significant phenomenon, I had to find out if it would repeat itself. I needed to
go through the experiment again using another group of doctors,
to establish whether the links with Mars, Jupiter and Saturn
would be observable a second time.

This was easier said than done. I could not list just any doctors: they had to be doctors who had made a name for themselves in their work, who 'stood out from the mass' while not
having (yet) been nominated to the Académie de Médecine.
Finally, I settled on the *Dictionnaire National des Contemporains,*
edited by N. Imbert and published in three volumes between
1936 and 1939, which I was able to consult at the Archives de la
Seine.[4] I listed the names of *all* the famous doctors mentioned in
it; I wrote to the register offices to find out their hour of birth
and received a reply for 508 of them; I calculated the positions
of Mars and Saturn. Once again, my doctors 'chose' the rise and
culmination of these planets for coming into the world. Once
again, they 'avoided' being born when Jupiter was moving
through those sectors of the sky. You would have to be a
research worker yourself to understand my satisfaction in having
my initial results confirmed like this. The hours of birth – the
data I had been at such pains to collect – were worth all the
trouble. I had my reward for, by persevering, I had discovered
what was probably a significant scientific phenomenon.

My interest in astrological research quickened, painting and
tennis became hobbies. I decided to collect the birth data for
outstanding French people who had made a name for themselves
in sport, politics, war, the stage, or whatever. It was more than
likely that exceptional doctors were not the only ones to prove
susceptible to planetary influences, nor Mars, Jupiter and
Saturn the only planets to show them. All I had to do was work
– which I did.

Sticking to the method which had been so successful with
doctors, I relied exclusively on biographical dictionaries. These
were objective tools as well, in which the date and place of birth
were usually specified although not, of course, the hour of birth.
I quickly acquired the reputation of being something of a pest in
register offices throughout the land, and particularly in large

towns where I had necessarily to make frequent inquiries to follow up the higher number of births. Sometimes I met with failure, but not often. It was my good fortune that the hour of birth has been recorded on birth certificates in France for a very long time, in fact, since a decision by the Committee of Public Safety in 1793. I blessed the French Revolution for that. Luckily, too, in France there is a law authorizing 'any applicant' to inquire about the hour of birth of any person, whether it is your father or the President of the Republic. Despite a chronic shortage of funds, I managed to get together in less than three years over 6,000 birth dates of famous French figures, distributed over ten professional groups. Then I worked out the astronomical calculations by hand.

It emerged that it was not only outstanding doctors who were born under a different sky from the ordinary run of mortals. The planet Mars, when positioned at birth in the sectors following its rise and culmination, favoured the success of sports champions and exceptional military leaders; Jupiter, in the same sectors, featured most frequently at the birth of actors and politicians. Where scientists were concerned – that is, members of the Académie des Sciences Française – it was Saturn which was dominant; on the other hand, artists – painters and musicians – presented an entirely opposite picture, since they 'avoided' being born when that planet occupied the key sectors of rise and culmination.

On a statistical level, these results (and many others which it would take too long to list in detail here) were entirely conclusive. The woman who was to become my wife encouraged me to publish them without further delay, and *L'Influence des Astres, Etude Critique et Experimentale* was published a year later, in July 1955.[5] I could not resist writing in somewhat polemical style and, from the moment it appeared, the book provoked various reactions.

Among the criticisms I received, one seemed to deserve particular attention. Or, rather, it was an expression of doubt: 'What would happen if you tried to pursue your observations outside your native country of France and no longer got any results?' In fact, the question had occurred to me, and it was a challenge which deserved to be met. A golden rule in science is always to question your own results; confrontation with the harsh realities of repeatability should not be avoided but sought after. The time had come to carry out my experiments in another country.

The United States seemed very far away to me then, and it was more sensible to begin with Europe. I finally settled on four countries, Italy, West Germany, Belgium, and the Netherlands, where information of the right kind would be most easily available. Since I could not get away during the year – I had to live, and that meant carrying out my profession as a psychologist – it was during the holidays that, with the help of my wife, I went gathering birth data in each of these countries, between 1956 and 1958. After many setbacks and the use of much cunning (we had a rule never to mention the word 'astrology', only 'demography', in our requests), we ended up with a collection covering over 15,000 dates and hours of birth – 7,000 for Italy; 3,000 for West Germany, where we encountered the highest number of refusals; 3,000 for Belgium; and 2,000 for the Netherlands. Some people, faced with this mass of information from *their* countries, made no secret of their incredulity and even doubt about its existence. Table 1 gives an extract from the data accumulated and later published.

These 15,000 births were not only of celebrities. They were all, of course, the birth dates of people who had been successful in their chosen professions, but only about half of them belonged to their actual elites. I had deliberately chosen them like that. Where the French data were concerned, I had noticed that a certain degree of success was necessary for the planetary effects to be visible. It is not sufficient just to be a doctor, sportsman or actor to produce that result. In my 1955 book, I gave several convincing examples. By putting together, where each of the European countries was concerned, well-known with less well-known figures in the same profession, I was in a position to verify again the influence of celebrity on the results. The second advantage was that I was able to assemble well-constructed control groups, since the little-known people belonged to the same professions and were born at the same times as the 'top men'.

All that was necessary now was to settle down and work out (by hand still, computers not being available then) the positions

Table 1   Extract from the list of German politicians, giving the date, hour and place of birth, and including the Nazi leaders Goebbels, Göring, Himmler

1903	GOEBBELS Joseph	29.10.1897,23h30	Rheydt -Rhld.-Pf.-
1904	GÖCKENJAHN Heinrich	30.9.1900,2h	Sellen b.Burget.-Nordrh.-Westf-
1905	GÖNNER Rolf (von)	25.4.1885,23h45	Arzberg-i-Bayern-Bayern-
1906	GÖRING Hermann	12.1.1893,4h	Rosenheim -Bayern-
1907	GREIM August	6.6.1895,22h	Helmbrechts -Bayern-
1908	GRIMM Friedrich	17.6.1888,18h30	Düsseldorf-Nordr.-Westf.-
1909	GROENEVELD Jacques	6.7.1892,7h15	Bundernee (ostfrieseld)-Nied-Sa.
1910	GUTENBERGER Karl	18.4.1905,12h	Essen -Nordrh.-Westf.-
1911	GUTSMIELD Franz	16.4.1901,19h	Grainet -Bayern-
1912	HABBES Wilhelm	13.3.1896,19h	Afferde über Unna-Nordrh.-Westf.-
1913	HAGER Heinrich	7.12.1893,21h45	Stadtsteinach -Bayern-
1914	HALLERMANN August	10.10.1896,13h	Hamm-Westfalen -Nordrh.-Westf.-
1915	HANFSTAENGL Ernst Franz	11.2.1887,5h	München -Bayern-
1916	HANSEN Hermann	21.7.1898,2h	Viöl über Husum-Schl.-Hol.-
1917	HARTMANN Erich	7.7.1896,11h30	Ludwigshafen-Rhld.-Pf.-
1918	HAUER Daniel	17.2.1879.23h	Bad Dürkheim -Rhld.-Pf.-
1919	HEINES Edmund	21.7.1897,16h15	München -Bayern-
1920	HEISZMEYER August	11 . Q.1897,22h30	Gellersen über Hameln -Nied.-Sa.-
1921	HELFER Wilhelm	26.12.1886,21h30	Kaiserslautern-Rhld.-Pf.-
1922	HELLMUTH Otto	22.6.1896,1h45	Markt Einersheim-Bayern-
1923	HELLWEGE Heinrich	18.8.1908,21h30	Neuenkirchen-Nied.Sa.-
1924	HELMICH Friedrich	21.6.1899,4h15	Hagen -Westf.-
1925	HENRICH Fred Fritz	4.5.1898,3h30	Aachen -Nordrh.-Westf.-
1926	HERBERT Willi	28.5.1904,21h	Frankfurt a.M. -Hessen-

Table 1 – continued

1927	HERGENRÖDER Adolf 2.8.1896,3h30 Bad Kissingen-Bayern-
1928	HESS Frotz 27.2.1879,20h Dannenfels -Rhld.-Pf.-
1929	HIDDESSEN Ferdinand 17.12.1887,12h30 Minden-Nordrh.-Westf.-
1930	HILDEBRANDT Richard 13.3.1897,2h30 Worms-Rhld.-Pf.-
1931	HIMMLER Heinrich 7.10.1900,15h30 München-Bayern-
1932	HINKEL Hans 22.6.1901,23h Worms a.Rhein -Rhid.-Pf.-

Source: M. and F. Gauquelin, *Birth and Planetary Data*, series A, vol. V (1970)

of the planets corresponding to the moment of the 15,000 new birth dates. Once I had made the calculations which, not surprisingly, took a little while, the critical moment came when I could judge whether the European research would confirm or invalidate the French results. The latter had been so clear that

Table 2   The planets of success in different professional groups*

after the rise and superior culmination of	high frequencies of births	low frequencies of births
JUPITER	actors and playwrights politicians military leaders top executives journalists	scientists physicians
SATURN	scientists physicians	actors journalists writers painters
MARS	physicians military leaders sports champions top executives	painters musicians writers
MOON	writers politicians	

* See notes 7, 8 and 10 for more details of the data summarized

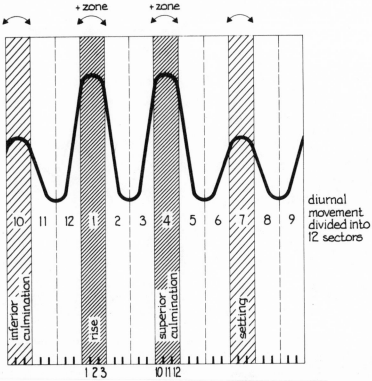

+ zone   + zone   + zone

diurnal movement divided into 12 sectors

inferior culmination

rise

superior culmination

setting

10 11 12 1 2 3 4 5 6 7 8 9

1 2 3   10 11 12

diurnal movement of planet divided into 36 sectors

Figure 3 Typical pattern of the intensity curve: if there were no planetary effects, the position of a given planet at birth would be random in any group of subjects; by observing the positions of planets at the birth of successful persons, we found that they tend to have planets related to their career in the 'plus zones' (also called 'key sectors'), or opposite those sectors where the effect is much less marked

Source: M. and F. Gauquelin, *Psychological Monographs*, series C, vol. II (1972)

they hardly allowed me any sort of fall-back position in case of failure. Every time a planet showed an abnormal frequency (either more or less often) in the key sectors of rising and culmination for a group of famous French figures, then Italian, German, Belgian and Dutch celebrities, too, ought to have been born under the same planet. On the other hand, this same planet, which was characteristic of the group of celebrities,

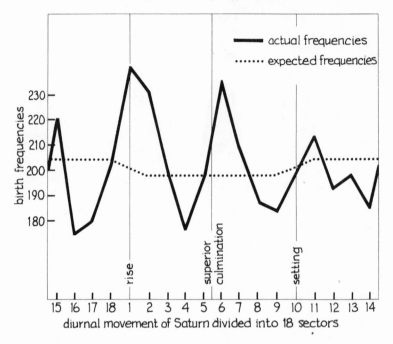

Figure 4　Distribution of Saturn for 3,647 physicians and scientists:
at the birth of scientists, Saturn appears to be more frequent after its
rise and superior culmination ('plus zones') than in the other sectors of
its daily revolution
Source: M. and F. Gauquelin, *Psychological Monographs,* series C, vol. II
(1972)

should be distributed in the control group – that is, those people
in the same profession, who were known little or hardly at all –
in the same way as it would in a group of ordinary births taken
at random. Those were the parameters of the problem.

The results of the European experiment turned out to be
quite remarkable. I attempted 13 repetitions of my French
observations using European data and, in every case, the results
observed for these births correlated with the French experiment.
Eleven times out of 13 the repetition showed significant statistical values. At the same time, as predicted, I found nothing
abnormal in the births of the control groups of little- or unknown people. This strongly reinforced the idea that these positive observations on the births of outstanding figures could not
be explained away by some arbitrary factor hidden from view,

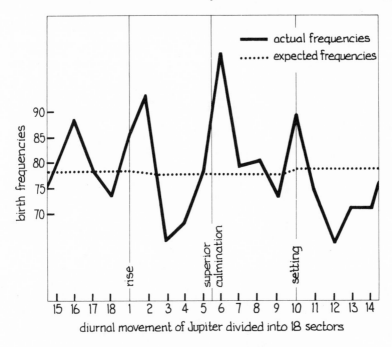

Figure 5 Distribution of Jupiter for 1,409 actors: at the birth of actors, Jupiter appears to be more frequent after its rise and superior culmination ('plus zones') than in the other sectors of its daily revolution

Source: M. and F. Gauquelin, *Psychological Monographs*, series C, vol. IV (1974)

otherwise I would have noted the same anomalies in the outstanding figures as in the others.

I published the full results of my European campaign in *Les Hommes et Les Astres,* which came out in 1960.[6] The dates and hours of birth of thousands of outstanding figures from five European countries (including France) furnished me with a solid basis for the reality of cosmic influence. After that, I increased the number of births in some of my groups and especially when, in 1970, my laboratory published all the birth and planetary data gathered since 1949.[7] Adding to the number of births has, as a rule, only served to improve the results.

The most interesting features of the observations are summarized in table 2.[8] Figures 3–6 show how the planetary frequencies present themselves in terms of diurnal movement. One

Table 3 Extract from birth and planetary data for successful Americans

Number	Profession	Name	Date and Time	Place of Birth		Planetary Position			
					Moon	Venus	Mars	Jupiter	Saturn
0129	MI, EX	BORMAN Frank	14.03.28, 19:30	Gary, IN	29	24	25	19	30
0130	AC	BOSCO Philip	26.09.30, 12:45	Jersey City, NJ	3	4	15	15	35
0131	AC	BOSLEY Tom	01.10.27, 00:36	Chicago, IL	24	32	28	12	24
0132	AC	BOTTOMS Timothy	30.08.51, 22:28	Santa Barbara, CA	25	24	26	3	21
0133	WR	BOURJAILY Vance Nye	17.09.22, 14:55	Cleveland, OH	17	9	1	11	12
0134	SP	BOURLAND Clifford	01.01.21, 18:10	Los Angeles, CA	27	15	15	30	30
0135	AC	BOUTON Jim (James Alan)	08.03.39, 20:50	Newark, NJ	35	27	31	23	19
0136	AC	BOVA Joseph	25.05.24, 18:15	Cleveland, OH	27	13	28	34	4
0137	SP	BOWDEN Don	08.08.36, 08:49	San Jose, CA	15	4	7	29	19
0138	X	BOWEN William Gordon	06.10.33, 15:07	Cincinnati, OH	28	10	9	14	36
0139	AC	BOWMAN Lee	28.12.14, 15:00	Cincinnati, OH	3	20	16	10	35
0140	SP	BOYD Bobby	25.10.33, 23:15	Chicago, IL	19	24	24	29	19
0141	SC	BOYER Paul Delos	31.07.18, 02:45	Provo, UT	3	34	23	35	29
0142	MI	BOYLAN George S.	03.12.19, 16:30	Wilmington, NC	4	21	23	27	25
0143	SC	BRADBURY Norris Edwin	30.05.09, 00:30	Santa Barbara, CA	16	27	1	19	33
0144	WR	BRADBURY Ray Douglas	22.08.20, 16:50	Waukegan, IL	4	14	7	15	14

ID	Cat.	Name	Date, time	Place					
0145	SP, PO	BRADLEY Bill	28.07.43, 11:20	Crystal City, MO	11	3	15	7	11
0146	PO	BRADLEY Thomas	29.12.17, 04:00	Calvert, TX	13	28	7	17	11
0147	SP	BRAGG Don	15.05.35, 15:20	Penns Grove, NJ	34	9	36	31	21
0148	MI	BRAND Vance DaVos	09.05.31, 02:20	Longmont, CO	2	34	21	24	5
0149	WR	BRANDI John	05.11.43, 19:58	Los Angeles, CA	10	25	36	28	35
0150	AC	BRANDO Marlon	03.04.24, 23:00	Omaha, NE	25	19	33	35	5
0151	SC	BRANSCOMB Lewis McAdory	17.08.26, 06:40	Asheville, NC	27	4	11	20	28
0152	X	BRAUER Jerald Carl	16.09.21, 23:45	Fond du Lac, WI	8	30	28	25	25
0153	SP, EX	BREEDLOVE Craig	23.03.37, 06:58	Los Angeles, CA	23	1	15	9	2
0154	MI	BREEDLOVE James M.	08.09.22, 09:00	Franklin, KY	21	36	31	2	3
0155	WR	BREMSER Ray	22.02.34, 00:01	Jersey City, NJ	16	30	26	4	28
0156	WR	BRENNER Elisabeth (DREW)	16.11.35, 03:10	Cincinnati, OH	7	36	27	30	22
0157	AR	BRESCHI Karen Lee	29.10.41, 21:38	Oakland, CA	11	21	8	3	5
0158	MI	BRETT Devol	01.08.23, 10:55	San Francisco, CA	20	9	8	34	1
0159	SC	BREWER Leo	13.06.19, 21:12	St Louis, MO	2	16	21	17	15
0160	AC	BRIDGES Beau	09.12.41, 03:56	Los Angeles, CA	9	29	22	15	17
0161	AC	BRIDGES Jeff	04.12.49, 23:58	Los Angeles, CA	10	24	36	23	36
0162	SP	BRODIE, John Riley	14.08.35, 03:20	San Francisco, CA	15	29	25	25	13
0163	AC	BROOKES Jacqueline V.	24.07.30, 18:50	Montclair, NJ	17	14	23	19	1
0164	WR	BROOKS Gwendolyn	17.06.17, 13:00	Topeka, KS	12	9	12	13	7

Source: M. Gauquelin, *Report on American Data*, series D, vol. X (1982)

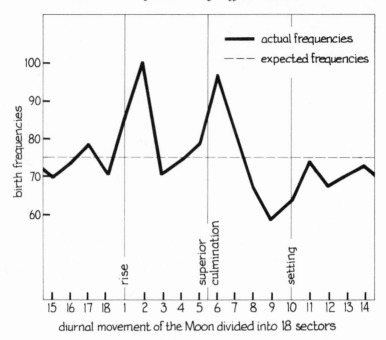

Figure 6 Distribution of the Moon for 1,352 writers: at the birth of writers, the Moon appears to be more frequent after its rise and superior culmination ('plus zones') than in the other sectors of its daily revolution
Source: M. and F. Gauquelin, *Psychological Monographs*, series C, vol. V (1977)

can see that, while the most crucial anomalies are observed when the planet is on the rise or going through its superior culmination, the regions of setting and of inferior culmination also tend to exhibit the same characteristics, though to a much less marked degree.

The effect of the probability of the results and the fact of frequency curves, meant that my observations contained enough to convince the most sceptical.[9] As far as I was concerned, there was not much left to prove about the relationship between planets and professional success. It was now up to others to judge the value of my work and to find the flaw, if there was one. The 'others' in question have not stinted themselves in trying to do so, but I will talk about that later in the book.

I finally went to the United States and lived there from

October 1979 to August 1980. I couldn't resist adding the births of outstanding Americans to my figures to see if the same planetary effects could be observed on the other side of the Atlantic. Despite the enormous difficulties involved in finding out hours of birth from the register offices, I managed to collect data on 1,400 outstanding people, distributed over several small groups (actors, sports champions, politicians, etc.). Table 3 shows an extract. I published the results in 1982: they confirmed, on a minor scale because of the size of the groups, the observations recorded in Europe.[10] However, I will discuss my American research at greater length in chapter 3.

Before that, I must explain how the laws of genetics and heredity interfere with planetary positions, to further complicate the puzzle of cosmic influence.

2

Enter Heredity

I must admit, I had no idea what caused the extraordinary results obtained from my collection of birth and planetary data. I let them carry me along, fuelling my enthusiasm for presenting the most solid possible proofs. To try to explain it all seemed a waste of time. But it did occur to me that the observations themselves might be a bit wild. I had shown a certain blithe unawareness in hoping to obtain them. And since, up till then, that way of operating had worked very well, I soon decided on a different type of experiment, which might reveal another aspect of cosmic influence. I wanted to test the hypothesis that there was some sort of astral heredity.

This idea has run through astrology for 2,000 years, from Ptolemy to the present day, owing a good deal more to esoteric speculation than to scientific reasoning. Kepler maintained that people's horoscopes resembled those of their parents, because the souls of both are in sympathy; this mysterious accord explains the resemblance of their horoscopes just as it explains that of their faces or personalities. By giving a detailed account of his horoscope and comparing it with his mother's, Kepler was able to understand a great deal about himself and his destiny which, according to him, this curious cosmic connivance would explain.[1]

At the beginning of the twentieth century, the French astrologer, Paul Choisnard, tried to give a scientific formulation to the belief. In his book, *La Loi d'Hérédité Astrale*, he asserted that children were often born with the Sun, the Moon or the ascendant in the same sign of the zodiac as their father or mother, and that this did not occur between people without links of kinship.[2] He also described the presence of certain planetary configurations, such as the aspects of certain stars, which turned up from one generation to another in the horoscopes of members of the same family. Some 30 years later, the Swiss astrologer, Karl E. Krafft, claimed in his *Traité d'Astrobiologie* that he had made more or less exactly the same observations.[3]

Was Kepler right? Although it was fairly vague even in the minds of its advocates, this notion of astral heredity had something fascinating about it. It had the additional merit that it could be researched through the birth dates of any man or woman, not just outstanding people. Yet, as early as 1955, I had discovered that the 'laws of astral heredity' proposed by Choisnard and his followers were, unfortunately, completely worthless.

In 1950, I had undertaken a series of experiments to check these so-called laws. Working on birth populations ten times larger than Choisnard's, I reluctantly came to the conclusion – verified several times since – that there did not exist any sort of zodiacal similarity between the horoscopes of parents and of their children.[4] So Kepler was wrong when, in 1598, he tried to convince Master Malin of the reality of astral heredity: 'Behold the kinship of births. You have a conjunction Sun–Mercury, so has your son; you both have Mercury behind the Sun. You have a trine from Saturn to the Moon, he has almost a Moon–Saturn sextile. Your Venus and his are in opposition . . .'

The laws of astral heredity, as applied to the traditional horoscope, may well be false, like so many other astrological beliefs. But it doesn't necessarily follow that one has to reject any sort of connection between genetics and the planets.

So I did, in fact, take up the idea, but gave it an entirely new slant by linking it with my observations on the professions. Although there might not be any astral heredity general to every horoscope, there could be a planetary influence on heredity which was limited to the rise and culmination of the planets. I can't begin to explain how such a thought occurred to me, except that I wanted to enjoy myself with the experiment and to

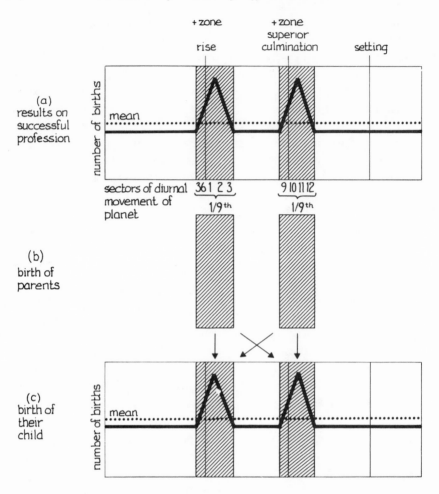

Figure 7   Planetary effect of heredity: astronomical conditions of the hypothesis
Source: M. Gauquelin, *L'Hérédité Planétaire* (1966), p. 93

feed my appetite for research from other sources, now that there seemed very little left to prove as far as the planets and professions were concerned.

At the same time, I had an extremely precise working hypothesis with which to test the alarming possibility of a correlation between planet and heredity (see figure 7). It was based on the results obtained on outstanding people (figure 7a). I reasoned that, in order to prove the existence of planetary heredity, there would need to be a frequent similarity in the positions of the planets, during their daily movements in the solar system, for the births of parents and children. But how should one define 'similarity of planetary positions'? My work on the professions offered the answer. In simple terms, a planet has a different effect on births when

it is in the zone which follows the rise or the zone which follows the culmination;
it is in any other zone in its daily movement.

I therefore formulated the necessary conditions for assessing the existence of planetary heredity in the following way: 'When, at the birth of a parent (whether father or mother), a planet was found in one of the two zones of rise and culmination (figure 7b), the child should preferably also be born when that planet was on the rise or at the culmination (figure 7c). And inversely, when the planet was found at the birth of the parent outside the zones of rising or culmination, then that should most frequently be the case with the child also.'[5]

All this, you might say, is very abstract, but it is essential to understand it. To take a practical example, my mother was born at Rouen in Normandy on 15 July 1900 at 4 o'clock in the afternoon, just at the rise of Jupiter. I was born on 13 November 1928 at 10.15 in the evening in Paris, at the culmination of Jupiter. In both cases, Jupiter was to be found in one of the key zones of the sky, and one could say that there is planetary heredity, as far as Jupiter is concerned, between my mother and myself. My sister was born in Paris on 9 October 1934 at 5 in the evening. Jupiter at that time was neither at the rise nor the culmination, and the hypothesis of Jovian heredity between my sister and my mother has not been confirmed.

This example should make my formula more comprehensible. But it also shows that a far-reaching statistical survey, comparing thousands of parents' birth times with those of their children, would be necessary before one could be at all certain about planetary heredity. One case, ten, or even a hundred would prove nothing. So, once again, I had to go back to primary material, gathering dates and hours of birth. At first sight it seemed less of a problem, as I could work on any birth dates, not just those of outstanding people. But in fact, there were two difficulties to be overcome, both of them considerable.

The first concerned access to the birth certificates of an area. We wanted to list data over a fairly extended period of time, but such consultation of the registers was forbidden to the public, for perfectly understandable reasons of discretion. In order to obtain special authorization, I had to resort to various ruses, including the old excuse of 'demographic research'. In this case, in fact, Françoise Gauquelin completed a thoroughly 'official' inquiry into the daily rhythm of births, which was subsequently published. This work led to fundamental conclusions about the evolution of the rhythm of births in relation to obstetrical policy, and was also essential for all future research on the influence of the planets.[6] I will return to it at the end of the book.

A birth certificate provides all the necessary data for the child concerned. But the parents remain a problem, at least, the parents of children born before 1923. That was our second difficulty. On the other hand, from 1 January 1923 French law had the good sense to demand the place and date of birth of its parents on the child's birth certificate. All that remained was to find out the hour of birth of each parent, from the office of the place where they were born. Once again, I congratulated myself on my good fortune in working in France: unbeknown to them, French law-makers since the Revolution had done much to aid my inquiries into cosmic influence. In some Paris suburbs we even managed, after enormous effort, to go back further in time for the birth data.

Actually collecting all the material involved hours of drudgery in register offices, voluminous correspondence and heavy expenditure. But in the end we had assembled over 30,000 dates and hours of birth for parents and their children, with the potential for some 15,000 comparisons between the skies at their respective births.[7]

Then followed, according to a well-established pattern, the calculation of the planetary positions – a task still carried out entirely by my own hand. I had decided that all the astronomical calculations should be done twice, which meant more than a year of work and held back publication of the data. I also had to be careful not to allow the results to influence me, even subconsciously. The birth dates of the parents and children were written one above the other on the same card, and I had a strip of cardboard (which I have kept as a souvenir) to cover up the planetary information about the parents when calculating that of the children. (During the winter of 1979–80, the computer at Astro Computing Services, San Diego, California, carried out the same calculations several thousand times faster than I had been able, and showed that I had been working the right way.)

I was rewarded for my trouble. The results, published in 1966 in my book, *L'Hérédité Planétaire*, showed up the effect of a planetary similarity between parents and children, as I defined it. Eleven years later, this planetary heredity was confirmed by myself and my collaborators after a second investigation into more than 30,000 birth dates of parents and children, the results of which were published by my laboratory (see figure 8).[8] In the 'absurd' field of cosmic influences, you can never prove too much and, thanks to this collection of over 60,000 births, I was in a position to describe fairly precisely what I called 'the planetary effect on heredity'.[9]

Children have a tendency to be born when a planet has just risen or culminated, if that same planet was in the same regions of the sky at the birth of their parents. Certainly, it is not a very pronounced tendency; yet, bearing in mind the great number of births examined, the probability that chance should have produced so many planetary similarities from one generation to the next falls to less than a million to one.

Nevertheless, this effect is only observed in relation to planets which are most massive and closest to us in the solar system – the Moon, Venus, Mars, Jupiter and Saturn – the ones we can easily make out with the naked eye, and exactly those ones for which effects were earlier recorded concerning outstanding people. No hereditary similarity was observed for the planets further away from us – Uranus, Neptune, Pluto, and Mercury, the smallest planet in the solar system. Interestingly, I had only ever received negative results about the effect of these planets on professional success.[10]

There were other notable features about the planetary effect on heredity. First of all, it did not depend on sex. Hereditary similarities were as frequent between father and children as between mother and children. In the same way, the statistical tendency was distributed with equal effect between boys and

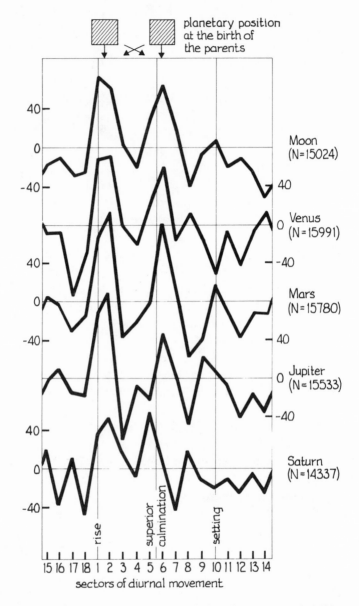

planetary position
at the birth of
the parents

Moon
(N=15024)

Venus
(N=15991)

Mars
(N=15780)

Jupiter
(N=15533)

Saturn
(N=14337)

rise

superior culmination

setting

15 16 17 18 1 2 3 4 5 6 7 8 9 10 11 12 13 14
sectors of diurnal movement

Figure 8 Planetary similarity at the births of parents and children:
results of the 1966 and 1976 experiments, according to the mathematical hypothesis in figure 7
Source: M. and F. Gauquelin, *Replication of the Planetary Effect in Heredity,*
series D, vol. II (1977)

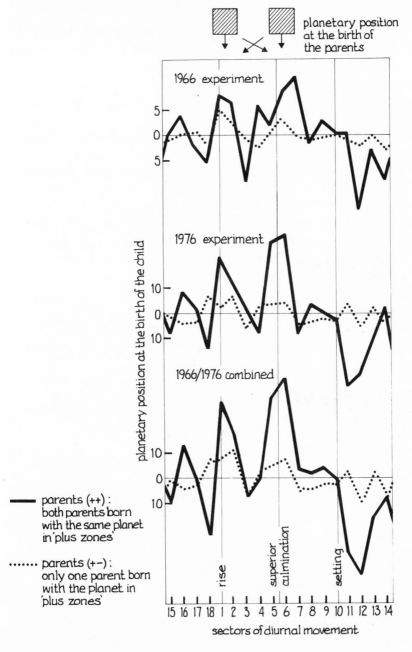

Figure 9 Increase in the planetary effect on heredity for children whose parents have the same planetary positions: combined results of the five significant planets
Source: As figure 8

girls. Moreover, if both parents of the child were born at the rise or culmination of the same planet, the tendency in the child was doubled (see figure 9). But planetary heredity becomes weaker over the generations and is less marked from grandparents to grandchildren, for instance. So all the evidence points to a planetary effect of hereditary origin, which does not go against the classic laws of genetics. Undoubtedly, my most interesting discovery was the way in which all planetary effects on heredity disappeared in children whose births did not occur naturally – that is, whenever there was surgical intervention (a Caesarean), or whenever the birth was stimulated or accelerated by the administration of drugs. This result is fundamental to understanding the effects of the planets, as well as being significant for the future of 'neo-astrology' and modern techniques of delivery 'by appointment'. I will return to the subject at the end of the book.

The demonstration of a planetary effect on heredity marked an important stage in my work. It was a watershed between my earlier observations on professional success and the later ones on character traits. It also opened up new horizons to me, although I had no clear idea about what happened at the moment of birth or in the instants which preceded it. I was led to consider the daily position of a planet at birth as the expression of one of the factors of heredity. Being born with such and such a planet in such and such a position in the sky is not simply a matter of chance: it is also a question of heredity. That was the crucial discovery.

The fact that my mother and I were both born when the planet Jupiter was in one of the key sectors was probably no mere coincidence. My mother had in all likelihood transmitted to me some genetic factor, which was objectivized by the similarity of the natal position of Jupiter. What was this genetic factor? It was clearly important, and it was up to me to try and define it. Between the relation of planet to professional success and the relation of planet to heredity there must be some sort of common denominator: call it the predisposition of the personality. That was the challenge I now had to meet, of solving the equation, transforming the hypothesis into scientific proof.

3

50,000 Character Traits

At the end of the 1960s, I was both satisfied and dissatisfied. I was pleased to have shown that the results concerning the link between planets and professions were reproducible from one country to another, to have mastered the complex methodology involved and to have demonstrated another important phenomenon, the relation between planets and heredity. Yet, at the same time as trying to find other researchers prepared to control my observations (I will discuss this later on), I wanted to strike out for new territory. My wife was ready for a rest from our labours but, for me, there was no alternative except to go further, if that were possible, with my experiments.

Throughout my study of the planets and professions, I had really been looking at a false resemblance, and the structure of the results suggested the underlying presence of another, stronger relation – that between character traits and the planets. More or less confusedly, it is true, I had started with professions, not only because they were convenient and objective as concepts, but also because they are associated with certain kinds of behaviour. Although there are fundamental psychological tendencies which lie behind success, the same type of personality does not succeed in the same way in every profession. In the course of my work as a psychologist, I had noticed that we all have a fairly clear idea about the character traits necessary for achievement in a particular profession, and my impression was confirmed in a study made then.[1] Most people would agree that an artist tends to be a dreamer, a writer imaginative, a politician a good talker, for instance, even if there is an element of stereotyping in these portraits. Popular common sense is at one with psychologists on this point, that every profession has a more or less clearly defined psychological profile. Of course, it's quite possible for a non-aggressive sportsman to become a champion, or for an introverted actor to become a film star; there are famous examples of it happening. But it is more difficult for them, and they are only the exceptions which prove the rule.

On this basis, it was not a very original idea to assume that sports champions would prefer to be born at the rise or culmination of Mars, or actors of Jupiter, since Mars has something to do with energy and Jupiter with extroversion. I had the beginnings of a hypothesis and I wanted to test it as quickly as possible. Doctors were intervening more and more in the natural process of childbirth, particularly since the 1950s, and, at the very least, I knew that the planetary effect on heredity was halted by modern obstetrical practices. There was a risk that the information available from the natal planet about the personality of the child would soon be destroyed, and I judged it urgent to describe the probable relations between planetary and personality factors before it was too late.

I had no idea how to go about tackling this inquiry. In 1966, I wrote: 'Today there is an almost insurmountable difficulty which prevents us establishing a typology of character based on reliable planetary observations. That is why we must, *provisionally*, leave the problem without any definitive solution.' But I continued: 'There is one way it could be tackled. We could go back over our professional figures and, using biographical information, make objective assessments of their personalities in terms of the positions of the planets at their birth. But such a huge undertaking would need a team of researchers, and a lot of backing.'[2]

That was a solution – to work on the personality traits of outstanding people – but whether it was possible or feasible to turn this experimental idea into an objective way of working was another matter. During 1967, the project matured in my head, and I decided that it must go ahead without delay, despite everyone's attempts to dissuade me from such a laborious task. I resolved to find some way of transforming it into a properly scientific investigation. It was an ambitious aim: I wanted to prove scientifically that the true correlation lay not in the relation between planet and profession, but in the relation between planet and personality; and I also needed to find a scientific way of describing these planetary personality factors. To achieve this twofold goal, I intended using the biographies of the outstanding professional people, for whom I had already collected all the birth data and planetary positions. The methodological tool I gradually worked out during 1967–68 and will now describe.[3]

Character traits form the basis of a psychology of the personality. As the psychologist, Jozef Cohen, has remarked: 'The language has spawned a proliferation of words, a deluge of description, in an attempt to name an infinity of personality segments.'[4] But ordinary speech is not the language of science. The psychologist, for his part, is trying to work scientifically and, according to the American psychologist, G. W. Allport, 'the nature of his work forces him to seek out and to identify dynamic mental structures and sub-structures (habits, needs, sentiments, attitudes or traits) *and to name them.* Mathematical symbols cannot be used, for they are utterly foreign to the vital functions which the psychologist is dealing with. Only verbal symbols (ambiguous and troublesome as they are) seem appropriate.'

Allport himself, in collaboration with H. S. Odbert, wrote a monograph which has remained a classic, providing a list of 17,953 words in the English language denoting character traits. In the preface, the authors explain the scientific application of their work which has, in fact, formed the point of departure for several psychologists examining the structure of personality: 'Sooner or later every psychologist working in the field of personality collides with the problem of trait-names. Whatever method he employs, he is forced to ask himself if the terms he is using in describing qualities and attributes of personality do actually denote psychic dispositions or traits, or whether these terms are mischievous verbal snares tempting him into the pitfalls or perils of "verbal magic".'[5]

To resolve this delicate problem, we need first to define our terms. What is a character trait? There are numerous definitions – for once, in agreement. A character trait is:

a relatively persistent and consistent behaviour pattern manifested in a wide range of circumstances;[6]
any enduring or persisting characteristic of a person by means of which he can be distinguished from another;[7]
a characteristic form of behaviour more generalized than the single reaction of simple habit. It should be regarded as a generalized habit and as a 'prominent' determining tendency in behaviour.[8]

Words used for a true character trait can be distinguished from those which denote a passing form of conduct. For instance, a habitually *optimistic* man may find himself momentarily *saddened* by the loss of a dear one. *Optimistic* is a character trait because it is a permanent attitude in this man, whereas *saddened* is not because it is a transitory state set off by an external stimulus. This is an important distinction. Indeed, among all the qualifiers in the language, there are only a relatively small number of words which designate true character traits.

How, then, do we define a personality type? A language is very rich, and some terms in it may have a closely related meaning (for example, happy-merry) or an entirely opposite meaning (for example, happy-sad). The first are synonyms, the second antonyms. Dictionaries of synonyms and antonyms are often used by psychologists. There are also words which, without really being synonyms, are associated with each other when describing a particular personality: 'One man may characterize a friend as *cautious*, a second may consider him *timid*, a third thinks he is *cowardly*. Obviously each is trying to represent a situation that all three recognize as existing within the personality in question.'[9]

This body of associated words characterizes the personality type. The researcher's aim is to discover, using the appropriate techniques, the constant relationship that may exist between certain traits. The groups which are thus built up make it possible to describe a limited number of personality factors within the diversity of personalities. In literature one can find excellent descriptions of personality types. More recently, psychologists have attempted to replace empirical observation with clinical examination and statistical experimentation, in order to pin down certain 'dimensions of personality'. Several of these studies have been published, of which the best known are probably those by H. J. Eysenck and R. B. Cattell.[10] All these authors have used character traits in their investigations, whatever method they may have adopted (biography, peer-group opinion, questionnaires, tests, etc.).

This is a rather didactic explanation of the importance of character traits in contemporary scientific study of the human personality. But it serves to justify my feeling that the character trait was the surest way of judging my hypothesis – that the natal position of a planet during its diurnal movement has a relation to particular personality types.

As a general source of information on character traits, I decided to use biographical accounts. This is one of the methods currently employed in personality psychology and seemed to offer two distinct advantages – objectivity and ease. In the first place, the biographies were written and published by others than myself, and with other aims in view. In the second place, I would be dealing with the biographies of people I had already studied. The fact that I had already published their natal and planetary coordinates[11] incidentally gave a further guarantee of objectivity, since I was bound not to deviate from a specific list of people: I could not be tempted to tip the scales in favour of my hypothesis, by including at the last moment this or that new case.

All that remained was to find a way of extracting the character traits from the biographies, so that I could apply them objectively. A short biography will illustrate my method. It is a piece written by a journalist about the French writer, François Mauriac, winner of the Nobel Prize for Literature:

One of the most striking characteristics of this long career was the impetuous curiosity which made him turn towards journalism, where he rapidly became notorious. Irritated, and irritating to others, with a fierce, impulsive and tireless pen, he soon made of his 'Bloc-notes' a sort of institution where his attitudes, his enthusiasms and even his wilful cruelty could be expressed without let or hindrance. Politically, his activity was modelled on his changes of mood and on his passions. It was a career which made of François Mauriac one of the 'personalities' of the literary world, whose books were looked forward to, whose witticisms were quoted, whose attacks provoked attacks to which he responded with inexhaustible energy, and which also, inevitably, received numerous official blessings.[12]

This little portrait, however lively it may be, cannot be used as it stands in a statistical investigation. So I extracted from it the character traits and behaviour attributed to Mauriac by the author, stripping the article in order to build up a telegraphic picture which could be used along with thousands of others in my huge inquiry. The result ran – curious, impetuous, irritated, irritating, fierce, impulsive, tireless, enthusiastic, cruel, expressed himself without let or hindrance, changeable moods, passions, a 'personality', made witticisms, attacks, energetic, sought official blessing.

For each character trait, such as 'curious', 'impetuous', 'fierce', I made a separate card and wrote on the same line Mauriac's name and the positions of the planets at his birth. I repeated the same procedure for other well-known personalities, by consulting articles and biographical material. For instance, from the biography of Cassius Clay (Mohammed Ali), published in *Current Biographies* in 1963, I obtained the following character traits – 'self-confident, self-adulation, loud, likeable, handsome, intelligent, witty, hard-working, bravado, relaxed, sense of humour, spontaneity, disciplined life, ambition'. For this enormous project to be valid, I was careful to observe three cardinal rules – to choose homogeneous biographies; never to eliminate a biography because it did not fit my hypothesis; and to take into account all the character traits mentioned.

It is a long and tedious task to research thousands of biographies and the work, begun in 1967, took several years. Conditions were often difficult; for instance, when I was researching sports champions and had to track down back numbers of a popular magazine of the inter-war period, *Le Miroir des Sports*. And when I had eventually located them, I had to copy all the details by hand, in the gloomy garret where they were stored. Even then, I had only the raw data, which still needed processing. As far as *Le Miroir des Sports* was concerned, the first stage was to get someone to type out all my handwritten notes. Then the typescript was given to another person, who had to underline and transfer to index cards all the character traits associated with a specific champion. In order to maintain maximum objectivity, this delicate task was entrusted to a psychology student who had not been told of the 'neo-astrological' hypothesis behind it all.

In this way, a catalogue of the character traits of sporting champions was built up. All that remained was to find out from my earlier publications the exact moment of birth of the champions and to note down the planetary positions corresponding to this or that character trait. After various processes, this resulted in the 'finished product' which, with the help of statistical analysis, I would use to test my hypothesis. The table below gives an illustration for the trait 'courageous': it lists the names of the first champions to whom this trait was attributed by their biographies, with the position of the planet Mars at birth shown opposite.[13]

Name of champion	Mars sector at birth (12 sector division)
Abbes, C.	1
Allais, E.	1
Archambaud, M.	12
Anthoine, E.	6
Baffi, P.	5
Baratte, J.	7
Bartali, G.	1
Bastien, J.	4
Bernard, M.	9
Bobet, L.	6

Each trait in this list constitutes a unit, the trait-unit. Each trait-unit is associated with the position of Mars at the birth of each champion. In order to use this material in a statistical way,

each association between a trait-unit and the position of Mars
can be analysed with other associations between traits and the
planet Mars noted from other subjects.

All these methodological considerations may be rather less than
thrilling for the reader, but they are nearly finished. As far as
the investigation is concerned, it was no longer necessary to
study the position of Mars at the birth of all the champions, but
only of those who shared a particular character trait. To give an
example, instead of looking at the entire group of champions, I
single out only those who are 'courageous', giving 300 'courageous' champions, together with 300 positions for Mars. I then
concentrate on the key sectors of rise and culmination. Let us
say for a moment that, compared to the whole group of champions, the 'courageous' ones are born more often with Mars in
the key sectors, according to statistical tests. This would establish a direct and more precise relationship between the character
trait 'courage' and the position of Mars. I continue from observing the role of Mars in sporting success to demonstrating the
relationship between Mars and courage, and this second correlation should be more marked than the first. This, at least, was the
hypothesis I intended to test. The method, which I have just
demonstrated, was universal and could be applied to any character trait, to any group of people and to any of the planets.

Although my project was so ambitious, I still had to work
within a framework and set limits to its scope. For a start, I
narrowed the professional groups down to sporting champions,
scientists, actors and writers. There were good reasons for this
selection, as achievement in each of the four was linked to a
particular planet in a clearly defined way – Mars for sporting
success, Jupiter for success in the theatre or cinema, Saturn for
scientific success and the Moon for success in literature. The
fact that Mars dominates in sporting personalities should mean
that there are many more Mars types among them than among
the non-champion population; and the same applies to the other
planets and personality types.

Between 1967 and 1977 my team of researchers, my wife
(whom I had finally convinced of the interest of the project) and
myself assembled over 5,000 biographical documents about
some 2,000 famous people, making it possible for us to collect

altogether 6,000 character traits for sporting champions, 10,000 for scientists, 18,000 for actors and 16,000 for writers. Eventually, I had at my disposal an impressive catalogue of over 50,000 character traits, an almost inexhaustible mine with which to evaluate my hypothesis. At first, the results were all analysed by hand but, fortunately, I later had the precious help of Neil Michelsen, president of Astro Computing Services, San Diego, California, and their research director, Thomas Shanks. A highly complex informational programme was set up, which enabled us to process the collected data with speed and accuracy and minimize the inevitable human error.

In accordance with the policy of publishing a final analysis of material from my investigations, my laboratory brought out, between 1973 and 1977, all the data of our research into character traits.[14] Each monograph describes the method employed and the results, and includes a complete catalogue of the character traits and biographical references (see tables 4 and 5 for examples) – and each is as big as a telephone directory.[15]

It is high time to look at the results which are, after all, the most important element in any research. First, we tried to establish an objective definition of the typical profile of a sporting champion, actor, scientist and writer, by referring to the works of psychologists and others specializing in the four professions.[16] This was followed by a list of the traits representing, as accurately as possible, the typical champion, actor, scientist and writer.

Thus, we are told, the sportsman has to be energetic, tenacious, courageous, obstinate, to succeed; the champion has a 'will of iron'. The successful actor is most often described as elegant, vain, funny, talkative, theatrical and eccentric – in short, an outgoing and expansive person. The scientist should be scrupulous, quiet, methodical and precise – introspective, in fact. Finally, the writer will be more successful if he or she is sensitive, witty, subtle, impressionable, a dreamer, imaginative, communicative, but a bit capricious.

In the same way, we were able to put together 'anti-profiles' – the 'weak-willed' champion, the introspective actor, the expansive scientist or the writer who was not at all impressionable – and this gave rise to lists of opposite traits.

If my hypothesis had any foundation, it was the character trait

Table 4 Extract from a catalogue of traits: the beginning of the American trait-catalogue

ABRASIVE	*ACTIVE*	Walton B.
Cosell H.	Anderson J.N.	Wicker T.
Kleindienst R.	Armstrong N.	
Martin B.	Brooke E.	*ACUMEN*
	Brown E. G.	Rahnquist W.
ABSENT-MINDED	Browning J.	Zumwalt E.
Jensen A.	Debusschere D.	
	Delorean J.	*ACUTE*
ABSOLUTE	Diller P.	Duvall R.
Martin B.	Eagleton T.	
Walton B.	Fairchild J.	*ADAMANT*
	Fidrych M.	Coppola F.
ABSORBED	Foyt A. J.	Redford R.
Wyeth J.	Gagne V.	
	Goddard J.	*ADAPTABLE*
ABSTEMIOUS	Gronouski J.	Jordan H.
Hefner H.	Kael P.	
Scott D.	Mahan L.	*AD-LIBBING*
	Nelson W.	Bean O.
ACCESSIBLE	Rose P.	Roth P.
Borman F.	Schirra W.	
Bowen W.	Scott D.	*ADMIRABLE*
Bowen W.	Seitz F.	Helms R.
Salinger P.	Shapiro I.	
Simon W.	Simon W.	*ADMIRED*
	Starr B.	Delorean J.
ACCOMPLISHED	Taft R.	Donahue P.
Keaton D.	Tarkenton F.	Reed W.
Minnelli L.	Verdon G.	Shore D.
	Yarborough C.	
ACCURATE		*ADOLESCENT*
Wyeth J.	*ACTIVIST*	*(PERENNIAL)*
	Bean O.	Redford R.
ACCUSES OTHERS	Bergen C.	
Friedan B.	Berrigan D.	*ADROIT*
	Friedan B.	Anderson J. B.
ACERBIC	Hufstedler S.	Hartzog G.
Kael P.	Millett K.	
Paar J.	Smeal E.	

ADVENTUROUS	Hall F.	*AGGRESSIVE*
Ashley E.	Harris Fre.	Butkus D.
Collins J.	Hodgson J.	Casper B.
Cooley D.	Janov A.	Chandler O.
Griffin M.	Mayo R.	Channing C.
Kilmer B.	Morton R.	Charles E.
Perot H.	Rauh J.	Cowans D.
Perot H.		Debusschere D.
Phillips W.	*AFFECTATION(NO)*	Debusschere D.
	De Gaetani J.	Donahue P.
ADVICE(AN)		Drysdale D.
Whitworth K.	*AFFECTIONATE*	Fairchild J.
	Shore D.	Foyt A. J.
AFFABLE		Frazier J.
Baker H.	*AFFLUENT*	Gilligan J.
Ehrlichman J.	Schlafly P.	Gonzales R.
Fodor E.		Hall F.
Grey J.	*AFRAID*	Harrelson K.
Griffin M.	Gardner A.	
Griffin M.	Lilly B.	
Gronouski J.		

Source: M. Gauquelin, *Report on American Data*, series D, vol. X (1982)

Table 5 Example of character traits for one person, taken from various biographical sources

| PASTEUR Louis | – 555 (100)

   – Distant – irascible.

(Br 110 111)

   – Passionate – research worker – assured – tense – self-willed – self-willed – serious – severe – sad.

(E. Picard, Z 4 sup 53 – 1)

   – Research worker – creative – experimenter – pensive – co-ordination – not conceited – hard – self-willed – efforts – enthusiastic – likes family life – not mundane – not conceited – concentrated – concentrated – careful – selective – not mundane – indefatigable – passionate – not mundane – revolutionary in science – admirable.

(G. Daremberg, T 8 sup 5082)

Source: M. and F. Gauquelin, *Psychological Monographs*, series C, vol. III (1982), p. 341

that mattered, not the profession itself: so the planetary results should vary greatly, depending on whether one focused on the typical profile of the profession or on its 'anti-profile'. That was the effect borne out, with a remarkable degree of clarity, by the statistics.[17] At the birth of 'iron-willed' champions, Mars was twice as often present in the key sectors of rise and culmination as at the birth of 'weak-willed' champions. 'Outgoing' actors came into the world with Jupiter in the key sectors much more often than actors who appear less expansive. 'Introspective' scientists were born in greater numbers at the rise or culmination of Saturn, unlike the 'anti-scientists'. And 'sensitive' writers were born when the Moon was on the rise or at its culmination.[18] (See figures 10–13.)

In short, the list of character traits defining the champion as 'iron-willed', the actor as 'outgoing', the scientist as 'introspective', and the writer as 'sensitive' provided a ready-made description of the four planetary personality factors – that is, of Mars, Jupiter, Saturn and the Moon. It was this which I had hoped to demonstrate.[19]

Nevertheless, the demonstration remained incomplete. I had described each planetary temperament through subjects belonging to a *single* professional group, and could see a very relevant objection, which might be expressed: 'You have been influenced in drawing up your type lists for each profession because you knew in advance the planet that "governed" that profession. Your brilliant statistics may only reflect a false objectivity.' I could not deny that a pilot list for each profession was still difficult to justify totally, despite all my precautions.

On the other hand, I now had the means of silencing my detractors and reassuring myself of my own objectivity. The tools for this purpose were simply the lists of character traits and, since these had been published, they could serve as a reference check. All that was required was to prove that the same character traits were associated with the same planets, whatever professional activity the subjects were engaged in. I had asserted, for instance, that the planet Mars was associated with certain character traits which appeared frequently among sporting champions (courage, will-power, dynamism, etc.). If that were

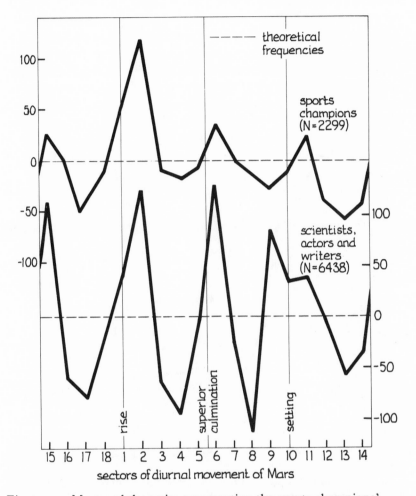

Figure 10 Mars and the traits representing the sports champions'
typical personality for sports champions and other groups of successful
professionals (see table 6): both curves show the same pattern – a
maximum of births when Mars has just passed the horizon and meridian, in particular after its rise and superior culmination ($r = 0.59$
$P < 0.01$). N indicates the number of trait-units
Source: M. and F. Gauquelin, *Psychological Monographs*, series C, vol. II
(1973)

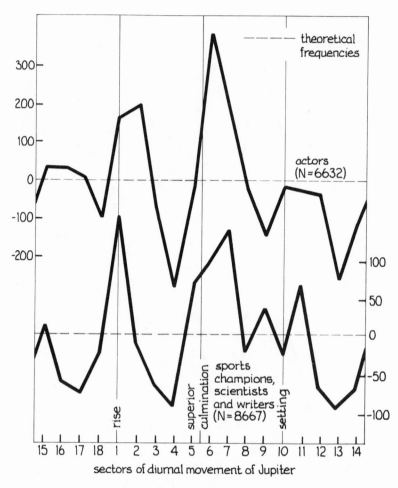

Figure 11 Jupiter and the traits representing the actors' typical personality for actors and other groups of successful professionals (see table 6): both curves show the same pattern – a maximum of births when Jupiter has just passed the horizon and meridian, in particular after its rise and superior culmination ($r = 0.78$ $P < 0.01$). N indicates the number of trait-units

Source: As figure 10, vol. IV (1974)

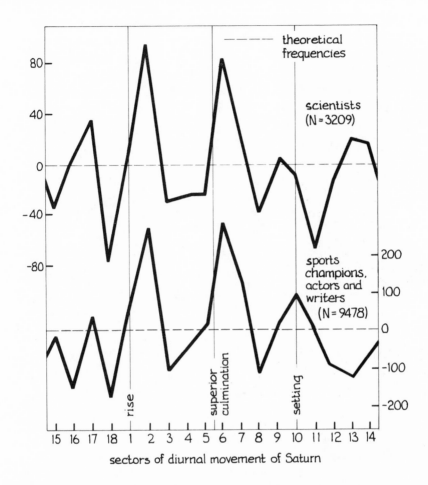

Figure 12 Saturn and the traits representing the scientists' typical personality for scientists and other groups of successful professionals (see table 6): both curves show the same pattern – a maximum of births when Saturn has just passed the rise and superior culmination ($r = 0.74\ P < 0.01$). N indicates the number of trait-units
Source: As figure 10, vol. III (1974)

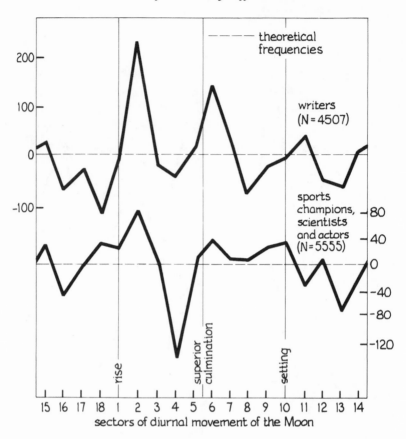

Figure 13 The Moon and the traits representing the writers' typical personality for writers and other groups of successful professionals (see table 6): both curves show the same pattern – a maximum of births when the Moon has just passed the rise and superior culmination ($r = 0.50\ P < 0.05$). N indicates the number of trait-units
Source: As figure 10, vol. V (1977)

true, then I should be able to find Mars associated with the *same* traits in actors, scientists and writers. The exercise could be repeated with Jupiter, Saturn and Moon personality types. In other words, not only 'iron-willed' sporting champions, but also actors, scientists, and writers with an 'iron will' should be born under Mars; 'expansive' personalities should be born under Jupiter; those who appear 'introspective' should be born under Saturn; and those with 'sensitive' personalities under the Moon.

If it were real, then the relationship between planet and character trait would remain constant throughout all the categories of person and profession.

As soon as the lists of Mars, Jupiter, Saturn, and Moon types were published (1973–77), I was in a position to demonstrate my hypothesis without anyone being able to reproach me with lack of objectivity (at least in this area). The demonstration took place in 1978, thanks to the 50,000 trait-units in my catalogue.[20] The relationship between planet and character trait could be observed without any need to take account of the professions. Persons with 'an iron will' often had a tendency to be born under Mars, the 'expansives' under Jupiter, the 'introspectives' under Saturn and poetic temperaments under the Moon. The existence of planetary types seemed to have been solidly established this time.

The Venus personality temperament remained a mystery. The 'Venus type' must exist, since I had observed positive results with regard to Venus in heredity, in the same way as for Mars, Jupiter, Saturn and the Moon. Children preferred to be born when Venus was rising or culminating if their parents were also born at the rise or culmination of Venus. It was thus a fair bet that the presence of Venus in the key sectors was related to certain character traits.

However, when I was investigating the professions, I had been unable to establish any clear correlation between Venus and success, doubtless because the Venus type was not linked to success in the professions which I looked at; other jobs might have provided more interesting results. Whatever the reason, I had to work out a substantially different hypothesis in order to describe the Venus type. Details of the method finally employed are given in a technical report.[21]

Our main idea was to find a way of successively separating the character traits. The first process was to extract from the catalogue of 50,000 trait-units all the traits where Venus was most frequently observed in key sectors. Most of these were far too brief to be of any use, whence the second process, of retaining as 'Venusian' traits only those attributed at least 50 times to our subjects. In this way, an initial profile of the Venus type began to emerge, although there were still some contradictions in the list. That led to the final stage, which involved using a dictionary of synonyms to eliminate objectively those traits where the meaning obviously didn't fit our tentative profile.

I hasten to say that this description of the Venus type has yet to be confirmed. It is not as complete nor as mathematically convincing as the planetary profiles established for the four preceding types. Yet it does provide specific elements which can be used to verify the Venus profile as soon as the occasion arises.

A catalogue containing 50,000 personality traits might be compared to a great cathedral organ, with a whole range of keys which can be played in a thousand different ways. Nevertheless, some notes recur more often than others under the organist's touch and, as they are in a musical register to which our ears are accustomed, sound pleasantly familiar. The same can be said of character traits. Some of the traits we 'played' appeared much more often than others in the biographies, just as they do in ordinary speech. On the other hand, rarely mentioned traits were valueless in isolation since they gave minimal statistical information, which is a pity because they were often highly descriptive; these could only be used when grouped within the 'Mars', 'Jupiter', 'Saturn' and 'Moon' lists already discussed.

So, having accumulated 50,000 trait-units in all, I could see that certain traits cropped up fairly frequently in the descriptions of our subjects. These included traits like 'modest', 'courageous', 'serious', 'ambitious', 'tenacious', 'authoritarian' – nearly a hundred altogether – and each was like a little statistic which could be examined separately.

The analysis of these 'isolated' traits, with all the professions mixed together, provided extremely useful information, permitting much more detailed investigation into the lists of the dozens of combined traits. The observations on two frequently attributed, isolated traits – 'strong will' (333 cases) and 'simple' (647 cases) – will serve as examples. 'Strong will' is a trait attributed especially to subjects born when Mars is on the rise or at the culmination (probability: less than 1 in 100,000), but *also* to people born with Jupiter in the same key sectors of the sky (probability: less than 1 in 1,000). On the other hand, it is rare to describe as having a 'strong will' a person born with either the Moon or Saturn in the key sectors (the respective probabilities being 2 in 1,000 and 2 in 100). (See figure 14.)

The trait 'simple' means 'without ostentation or affectation'. Biographies rarely attribute the description 'simple' to people born at the rise or culmination of Jupiter (probability: less than 1 in 100,000), while this personality trait appears very often in the biographies of 'Saturn' people (probability: less than 1 in 100,000). One is struck by the 'mirror image' distribution that occurs between Jupiter and Saturn. ('Lunar' people are not very often described as 'simple' either, but the observation was only marginally significant, and may well have been the product of chance.) (See figure 15.)

Looking at these two examples, it is easy to see how one can use a study of 'isolated' traits in order to build up a fuller description of planetary personality factors. That study is in the course of publication.[22]

My enthusiasm and curiosity were already aroused for the next project – that of assembling a picture of different planetary types, based on the biographies of famous people born not in Western Europe but on the other side of the Atlantic.

I mentioned briefly at the end of chapter 2 my investigation into outstanding Americans and the difficulties I had in obtaining their birth hours. However, I finally managed to collect 1,400 cases, which gave me a way of controlling, from the other side of the Atlantic, the existence of planetary types discovered on the basis of European celebrities. In theory, the exercise was a straightforward matter of getting together the biographies of the American people whose birth hours I had, following the same method as before, and seeing whether there was the same correlation between character traits and planets.

In practice, all that remained was to find the biographies, which could only be done properly on the spot, in the USA. While staying in San Diego, California, I worked at break-neck speed between January and July 1980. The surroundings were much more congenial than usual, but time was limited before my return to France. A further complication was that the birth certificates arrived in no particular order and I had to set about finding the biographical material haphazardly.

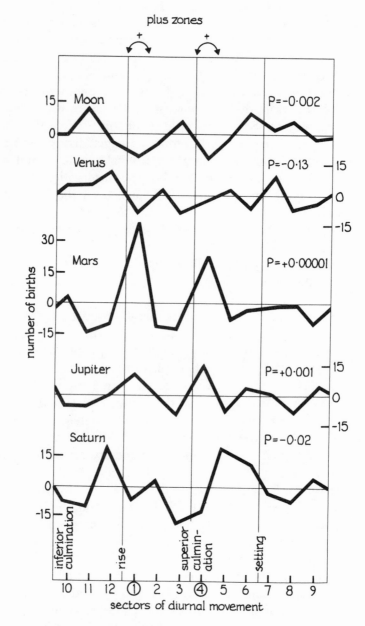

Figure 14   The character trait 'strong will' (*P* = probability for 'plus zones' 1 and 4, number of cases 333)

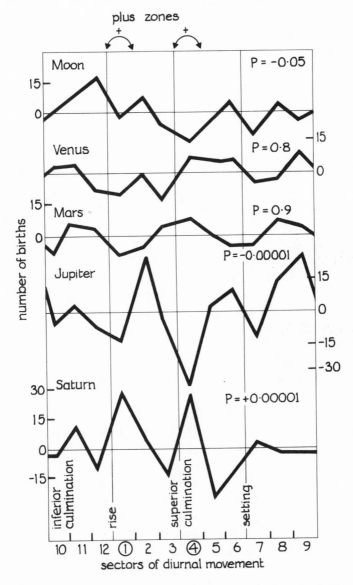

Figure 15 The character trait 'simple' (*P* = probability for 'plus zones' 1 and 4, number of cases 647)

I decided to limit my inquiry to certain documents, and to make photocopies which I could work on at leisure when I got back to Paris. One of the biographical series I used was *Current Biographies*, a monthly publication with a wide circulation in the USA, which provides short biographies of well known personalities, mostly Americans. All the professions were represented in it. I used *Current Biographies* from the first year of publication, 1940, up to and including May 1980, for material on all the people for whom I had a date, hour and place of birth. The second series was the *Lincoln Library of Sports Champions*, a popular publication in 20 volumes, giving brief biographies of all the most familiar American champions. This additional source was necessary because *Current Biographies* was relatively weak on sports champions – precisely the largest professional group in my American data. Moreover, my 'enemies' on the Committee for the Scientific Investigation of Claims of the Paranormal (CSICOP) had used it, before I had, to prove that the Mars effect on sports champions did not exist. I will expand on this later in the book.

Altogether, from these two sources I assembled the biographies of 500 people and, from them, extracted over 5,000 character traits. When I got back to Paris in the autumn of 1980, I hoped to find out as quickly as possible whether the same planetary types as had been described in relation to the European births would be evident in the American births. This time, Astro Computing Services did all the astronomical calculations.

The lists of Mars, Jupiter, Saturn and Moon traits, published some years earlier, dictated my analysis of the American data. In the American catalogue, I picked up systematically all the traits in the 'Mars' list. Then I noted the position of Mars in the sectors at the birth of each of the Americans who showed these traits. I observed exactly what I had hoped for: outstanding Americans described as having 'Mars' traits were born more often than others with the planet Mars in the key sectors of rise and culmination. I worked in the same way, and with the same positive results, on the Jupiter, Saturn and Moon lists and, even regarding Venus, the pilot list I had put together on the basis of our earlier framework seemed to show a fair degree of validity (see figure 16).

In short, planetary temperaments could be seen in American

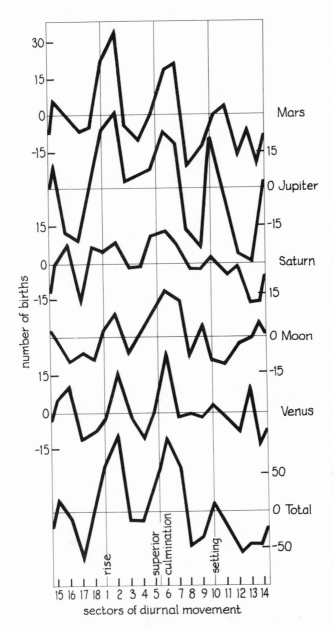

Figure 16 Character traits of well-known Americans: birth frequencies associated with several sets of traits at different periods of the planets' diurnal distribution (the lists of traits used for each planet are exactly the same as those we used before for our experiment on well-known Europeans)

Source: M. Gauquelin, *Report on American Data*, series D, vol. X (1982)

Table 6 Extract of twenty traits describing planetary types

Jupiter	Saturn	Mars	Venus	Moon
ambitious	cold	active	affable	amiable
authoritarian	concentrated	ardent	agreeable	disorganised
conceited	conscientious	belligerent	ambiguous	dreamer
gay	discreet	brave	attractive	easy-going
harsh	introvert	combative	beloved	fashionable
humorous	methodical	daring	benevolent	friendly
independent	meticulous	dynamic	charming	generous
ironical	modest	energetic	considerate	good company
lively	observer	fearless	courteous	good hearted
mocking	precise	fighter	elegant	helpful
prodigal	reserved	lively	flattering	imaginative
proud	sad	offensive	gallant	impressionable
show off	simple	reckless	gracious	impulsive
social climber	sombre	spontaneous	juvenile	merry
spendthrift	stiff	strong-willed	kind	nonchalant
talkative	taciturn	stormy	obliging	popular
warm	thoughtful	tireless	pleasant	socialite
well-off	timid	tough	poetic	spontaneous
witty	uncommunicative	valiant	polite	superficial
worldly	wise	vitality (full of)	seductive	tolerant

Source : Extracted from the much more detailed lists published in M. and F. Gauquelin, *Psychological Monographs*, series C, vols II–V and series D, vol. I (1973–78) celebrities in just the same way as in outstanding European people. The transatlantic evidence gave a degree of universality to planetary types, which could be found in people born in countries far apart. The results of my American research were published in 1982.[23] The monograph also included natal and planetary coordinates for all the subjects of the investigation, as well as the complete catalogue of the thousands of character traits found in the biographies of these people.

The so-called 'character trait' method makes it possible to assume that the passage of the planet following the horizon and the meridian is in general the expression of one particular type of temperament. I have attempted to describe the planetary types, bearing in mind that these profiles are still only provisional and suffer from the constraints established by my choice of method. These restrictions are mainly semantic, since ordinary language is not the language of science. Nevertheless, the lists of 20 traits defining Jupiter, Saturn, Mars, Venus and Moon types (given in table 6), form a good basis for future studies.

Is there any need to add that these planetary types do not explain the *entire* personality of an individual? They are only one among many important factors – education, environment, chance – that forge a personality and shape a destiny. There is nothing hypocritical in this proviso; it is not like the concluding paragraphs customarily written by scientists with disarming modesty. Quite simply, I am delighted with the way my search for planetary types has turned out. But I am conscious of all that remains to be done to sort out this tangle of facts.

A framework of planetary typology is a huge clearing in the uncharted forest of astral influences. But we have not reached the middle of the forest yet. If we are to achieve our aim, of crossing it from one side to the other, we shall have to solve all the problems and contradictions thrown up by research. One of these questions concerns 'complex' planetary temperaments. There are, in theory, 'complex' temperaments when not one but two or three planets occupy the key sectors of rise and culmination at the birth of a child. What happens then? To what extent do the influences of these planets combine?[24]

Another difficulty is that of character traits which, at the moment, appear on two lists simultaneously. There are, for instance, a certain number of traits which appear on both the Mars and Jupiter lists. I would like to decrease such cross-references as far as possible.[25] Experiments are in hand which could provide satisfactory solutions to these, and the thousands of other problems. It is my hope that the present sketch of a planetary typology will gradually develop into as perfect a diagram as possible.

4

Personality and the Planets

Backed by a wealth of figures taken from tens of thousands of character traits, I now had a planetary typology classifying people in five major categories – Mars, Jupiter, Saturn, Moon and Venus types. As a trained psychologist, I naturally wondered how such a classification would fit within the principles of psychology as taught in universities. I was well acquainted with the ingenious attempts of researchers, since the beginning of the century, to create a scientific psychology and, in particular, to arrive at some sort of objective description of the human being. Yet, by and large, they had taken no interest in astrology, unless to reject it as being implausible. For most of them, a planetary typology presented all the appearance of some antediluvian monster, risen from the depths of time to spread panic through the well-padded atmosphere of university psychology departments. The monster was refused entry to the laboratories. To me, it seemed only right and proper to build a bridge across the gulf separating modern theories of personality from the discovery of planetary temperaments.

Psychologists are highly imaginative people. They have described the human personality, using tests and questionnaires, but each in his own way. There was a wealth of choice. Moreover, the scientific status of personality classifications is not as clear-cut as, for instance, blood-groups in medicine. All doctors agree that there are four main blood groups in human beings –

A, O, B and AB. We are a long way from that sort of unanimity in psychology, where there are almost as many classifications of personality types as there are writers. Which should I choose in order to establish that link between their theories and mine?

I started off by eliminating any concept which lacked a well-defined, easily quantifiable basis, however interesting it might be in other respects – for example, psychoanalytical theories or theories of humanistic psychology. As the logician of science, Karl Popper, remarked, such concepts are not 'falsifiable'.[1]

Instead, I confined myself to classifications based on precise concepts, described in straightforward terms and leading to mathematical analysis of the experimental data. Two main theories of the structure of personality have, between them, the support of most psychologists – that of R. B. Cattell and that of H. J. Eysenck.[2] Both men put the results of tests and questionnaires through a refined statistical treatment of factorial analysis and then defined the human personality in radically different ways. For Cattell, there are 16 'factors' in a personality, whereas for Eysenck the 'dimensions' of the personality add up to only three. I have no intention of going into the polite, but intensely argued, polemics exchanged between these eminent scientists and their numerous supporters. However, my personal experience as a psychologist made me more sympathetic to Eysenck's ideas, which seem to bear a closer relation to psychological reality, doubtless because of the spirit of synthesis presiding over his theory.

For Eysenck, professor of psychology at the Institute of Psychiatry, University of London, the 'factors' put forward by his colleague Cattell were too numerous: there was too much correlation between them to be able to draw any real distinction. Was it not simply juggling with figures and outlandish words to distinguish, as Cattell had done, between factor A: cyclothymy ↔ schizothymy and factor H: audacious cyclothymy ↔ essentially inward-turned schizothymy? Eysenck at least admired Cattell's mathematical virtuosity in dividing the human personality into these excessively small fragments.[3]

Eysenck adopted a different factorial approach for the results of his personality questionnaires. First of all, he highlighted two

fundamental dimensions of the personality which can be objectivized in the form of four super-factors – introversion ↔ extroversion: first dimension; emotional stability ↔ emotional
instability ('neuroticism'): second dimension. These two dimensions have no correlation between them and are therefore, to use
the jargon of the factorialists, orthogonal factors. More recently,
with the help of his wife Sybil B. G. Eysenck, he has described a
third dimension of personality – tough-mindedness ↔
tender-mindedness ('psychoticism').[4]

Let us stay for a moment with the introversion ↔ extroversion dimension, which is doubtless the most well known.
Eysenck writes:

> The typical extrovert is sociable, likes gatherings, has a lot of
> friends, feels a need to talk to others and does not much like
> reading and studying alone. He likes taking risks and acting on
> the impulse of the moment. He enjoys jokes, is always ready with
> repartee and often wants to change activities. He is optimistic,
> does not bear a grudge, but is often aggressive and flares up
> easily. On the whole, he is not always well controlled and is not
> necessarily a dependable type.

> The typical introvert is calm, retiring, introspective. He loves
> books more than people. He is reserved and distant except with
> close friends. He tends to remain in the background and mistrusts
> momentary impulses. He avoids emotions, deals with everything
> in order and usually values a well-organized way of life. He does
> not show his feelings, rarely behaves aggressively and does not
> easily get angry. He is a reliable person, a trifle pessimistic, and
> with a strong belief in the importance of moral values.[5]

To me, it was blatantly obvious that the extrovert type resem-
bles the Jupiter temperament and, to a lesser degree, the Mars
temperament, while the introvert type is almost the exact image
of the Saturn temperament. There was an overwhelming tempt-
ation to work with Eysenck, and I first met him at the Institute
of Psychiatry in 1974 on one of my trips to London. I was
somewhat apprehensive about showing him my work, knowing
the mathematical rigour of his own research as well as his exact-
ing criticism of certain schools of psychology. Eysenck had an
independent mind: he did not share the opinion, widespread

among his colleagues, that astral influence is a subject without any sort of scientific interest. He listened with characteristic calm and concentration, asked me to leave some of the publications put out by my laboratory, and later wrote to request clarification of certain aspects of my method.

Eysenck's interest was awakened. In an article in *New Behaviour* in May 1975, he put forward certain hypotheses which, if they could be confirmed, would make it possible to associate the theory of planetary factors with his system of personality analysis.[6] He predicted, in particular, that introversion must be related to Saturn and extroversion to Jupiter and Mars. If no clear forecast could be made about 'neuroticism', there was good reason to hope for results with the new dimension of personality described by the Eysencks, that is, 'psychoticism'. 'Tough-minded' people should preferably be born under Jupiter or Mars and 'tender-minded' people should be born most often under Saturn. Concerning this 'psychoticism', Hans Eysenck was struck by an earlier observation of mine – the astonishingly high percentage of Nazi leaders in the Third Reich who had been born at the rise or culmination of Jupiter.[7] Famous Nazis not being renowned for their soft-heartedness, the association between Jupiter and the 'tough-mindedness' portrayed by the Eysencks sprang to mind.

These hypotheses were worth testing. The Eysencks, Françoise Gauquelin and I settled on a mode of working. To begin with, we sent Sybil Eysenck the alphabetical list of all the traits in our catalogue, and she classified some of these traits according to one of the six categories (introversion–extroversion, stable–unstable, tough–tender) in function of their psychological significance (see table 7 for an example from the American data, used in the later experiment). This initial process was quite objective, as Sybil had no idea of the planetary positions of the people to whom these traits were attributed. Her choice was guided solely by the desire to establish clusters which fitted as closely as possible the dimensions of personality described by her husband and herself. It was only after this first process of selection that the positions of the planets for the subjects in question were calculated.

After appropriate statistical treatment, the results of the inquiry were published in 1979 in the *British Journal of Social*

Table 7   Traits assigned by Sybil Eysenck for E +, E −, P +, P − dimensions from the American trait-catalogue

E+   active alert amusing animated animates others arguer athletic attractive bar brawling brisk carefree change (ability to) charming cheerful cheerleader communicative confiding conversationalist daredevil drive drug habit dynamic easy-going effervescent energetic enjoyment enthusiasm extravagant extrovert free friendships (keeps) fun-loving funny gay (merry) glib happy hasty hot-tempered humor (sense of) ill-tempered impetuous impulsive irregular irrepressible jokes jovial leader lively merry optimist organizer persuasive pleasure-seeker popular prankish protester quick rabetiasian reckless repartee risk (takes) rowdy satirical self-advertisement self-assured sensuous sociable solitary (not) spendthrift spontaneous successful talks easily talks much tireless unconventional verve vitality vivacious voluble witty

E−   accurate awkward confidence (lack of) friends (has few) introverted methodical nature (loves) parties (doesn't like) publicity (doesn't like) punctual quiet reads much reflective regular reserved restrained retiring self-confidence (lack of) self-control solitary talks (not much) unsociable.

P+   absent-minded aggressive ambitious arguer arrogant assertive belligerent bitter combative complainer conformist (non creative criticises daredevil defiant difficult to deal with distrustful drink-loving drug-habit egotism enemies (has) explosive extremist fearful fearless fierce fighter free (thinker) gamin hard-drinking hostile hot hot-tempered ill-tempered imposing impulsive individualist innovative leader loose machiavethian malicious militant offensive original persuasive pleasure-seeker polemic prankish protester quarrelsome rebellious reckless revolt risk (takes) solitary suspicious thruster tomboy tough unconventional unmannerly unsociable violent vulgar warrior wicked.

P−   accessible affable aggressive (not) friendly friendships (keeps) animal (loves) considerate homebody polite compassionate conscientious consciousness cooperative courteous feminine domesticity obedient.

E + extroversion; E − introversion
P + tough-mindedness; P − tender-mindedness
Sources: M. and F. Gauquelin and S. Eysenck in *Personality and Individual Differences* 2 (1981), p. 347; American catalogue of traits published in Michel Gauquelin, *Report on American Data*, 1982

and Clinical Psychology.[8] They confirmed the hypotheses advanced by Hans Eysenck in 1975, in all cases using the categories as defined by Sybil Eysenck. The 'introverts' were born far more often than chance would allow with Saturn in the key sectors of rise and culmination; the 'extroverts' chose to come into the world when Jupiter or Mars were in those zones of the sky. By contrast, the 'introverts' 'avoided' being born when Jupiter or Mars were at the rise or culminating, and the 'extroverts' 'avoided' being born when Saturn was going through those zones of the sky (see figure 17). The results also confirmed the hypotheses about 'psychoticism', which opposed 'tough-minded' – 'Nazis' one might call them, with exaggeration – to 'tender-minded' people. The 'tough' were born much more often under Jupiter and Mars than under Saturn, and *vice versa*.

All these observations were encouraging, but we concluded our article on a note of caution: 'Before thinking too much about possible explanations of our data, it may be wise to insist on replication.'[9] Fortunately, my recent work on character traits taken from the biographies of American people enabled us to renew our experiment with the Eysencks.[10] We could use the catalogue of 5,000 traits belonging to 500 outstanding Americans and follow exactly the same mode of operation as during the first experiment.

The results, published in 1981, in *Personality and Individual Differences*, show exactly the same correlations with the American data as with the earlier European data. The 'introverts' and the 'tender' prefer to be born under Saturn; the 'extroverts' and the 'tough' under Jupiter and Mars (see figures 18 and 19). The antediluvian monster of 'neo-astrology' has managed, for the first time, to get along happily with modern psychology.

But modern psychology demands more of neo-astrology. Until then, my description of planetary types had been based exclusively on the study of people who were highly successful and had shown themselves to have talent and character – the 'cream of the cream' among people, the highest rungs on the ladder of social values. In fact, I had been working in the opposite direction to the preoccupations of most psychologists. Most of the major psychological theories – those of Freud, to give an obvi-

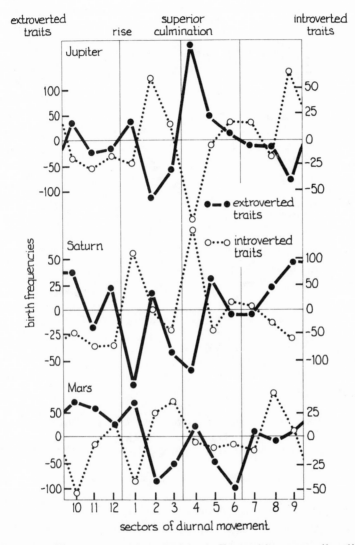

Figure 17 'Extroversion–introversion': Eysenck's personality dimen
sion and the position of the planets at birth, European subjects
Source: M. and F. Gauquelin and S. Eysenck in *British Journal of Social and
Clinical Psychology* 18 (1979), p. 73

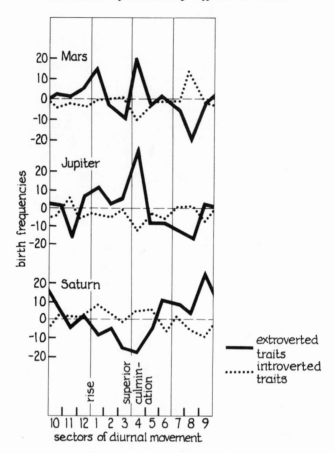

Figure 18 'Extroversion–introversion': Eysenck's personality dimen-
sion and the position of the planets at birth, American subjects
Source: M. and F. Gauquelin and S. Eysenck in *Personality and Individual
Differences* 2 (1981), p. 348

ous example – rely on the clinical study of mental disorders.
Tests and questionnaires are compiled on the basis of the data of
psychopathology before being applied to normal people. Like
medicine, the science of psychology has developed principally
by observing people right at the bottom of the scale of intellectual or character values – the dregs of society, the mentally
deficient, the mad and the criminal. The study of above-average
people has interested almost no one engaged in research in psychology laboratories. (Incidentally, one might ask why they

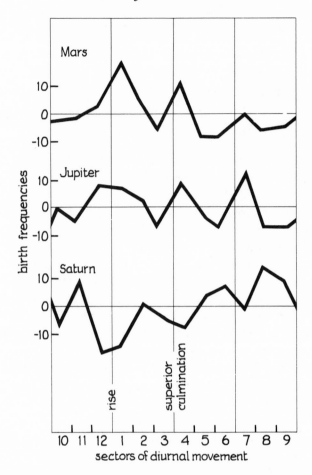

Figure 19 'Tough-mindedness' (psychotism +): Eysenck's personality dimension and the position of the planets at birth, American
subjects
Source: As figure 18, p. 349

could not contribute as much to the findings of psychology as
idiots and madmen.)

My approach had not been orthodox, in psychologists' terms,
and it seemed logical – indeed, imperative – to undertake a study
of the mentally ill and criminal. I had actually written: 'Murderers and psychotic people present extreme character traits
which are included in well-known modern classifications of
human personality (Cattell, Eysenck). It has also been argued

that there is no decisive break between normal and pathological personalities. People who are insane merely carry to extremes the pathological and morbid strains that are present in the most ordinary people.'[11]

In fact, I had been aware of the interest of this kind of inquiry early on in my research and had already taken steps in that direction. In 1951, I had permission to consult the police files of the Palais de Justice in Paris, and collected details of birth of 623 murderers, most of whom had ended up under the guillotine. Then in 1964, I managed to get authorization to consult the medical files of the Sainte-Anne hospital in Paris, the most important psychiatric hospital in the city. I assembled some 6,400 dates and hours of birth of mentally ill people, people suffering from schizophrenia, from various psychoses (manic-depression, hallucinations, alcoholism) and from nervous disorders.

I recently published the results based on this significant material of 7,000, together with the birth data.[12] But, except for one or two interesting observations, they are negative (see figure 20). There seems to be no justification for the hypothesis that murderers and psychotics have a tendency to be born under different cosmic conditions from those prevailing at the birth of 'normal' people. As far as I can judge, there is no planetary temperament which seems to be particularly related to some mental disorder or to a tendency to kill one's nearest and dearest. My assessment was:

> The outcome of this investigation leads us to the probable conclusion that the planetary effects discovered on the character traits of successful subjects do not apply for abnormal subjects. If it is so, abnormal psychology is not the field of planetary effects. It could be an important fact which needs to be understood in the framework of our researches. A possible explanation is that the biological disorders interfere with the normal genetic dispositions of the subject, modify his current behaviour and, sooner or later, impose a new pathological personality which takes the place of the normal one.[13]

A study of the 'bottom of the ladder' seemed to be of no benefit in advancing my knowledge of planetary effects.

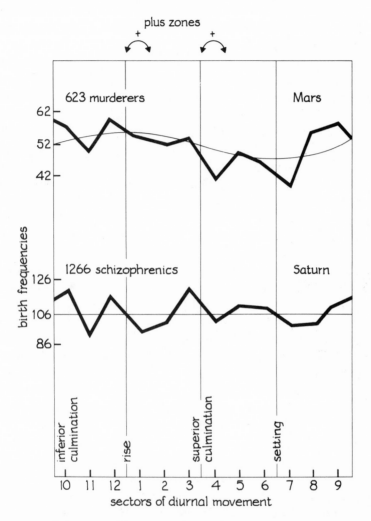

Figure 20   Crime, psychiatry and the planets, two examples of negative results: at the birth of murderers, the aggressive planet Mars is
distributed at random and, in particular, is not more frequent in the
'plus zones' of rise and culmination; at the birth of schizophrenics,
Saturn, the planet of withdrawal, is not more frequent in the 'plus
zones'
Source: M. Gauquelin, *Murderers and Psychotics*, series D, vol. IX (1981)

Between these two extremes, the 'cream' of famous people, and the rejects of society, lie the vast majority of people, the 'normal', 'ordinary' people, like you and me. What happens as far as they are concerned?

Common sense suggests that it would be exceedingly strange if planetary types were a prerogative of the elite. The four blood groups exist for ordinary people as they do for famous people. So why should one not equally find, among the anonymous crowd, the five planetary groups of personality – Mars, Jupiter, Saturn, Venus and the Moon? The practical importance of this question is self-evident for, if everyone can claim their planetary factor, the whole of psychology would gain from my observations.[14] The trouble is that 'ordinary' people have no biographies written about them. I lacked the tool I had made for myself – the method of character traits – which had succeeded so well with famous people.

Fortunately, there was clinical observation, which was a useful way of getting an idea of experiments to be undertaken. And the clinic, as far as I could see, was weighted very favourably towards a planetary psychology of 'ordinary people'. Some of my colleagues, considered to be very critical and authoritarian, were born under Jupiter; such and such a member of my family, known for discretion and reserve, was born under Saturn; and as a competitive tennis player, I had seen how difficult it was to wrest final victory from those opponents who had Mars as a dominant planet.

But that is merely anecdotal and perhaps valueless: it is so easy to delude yourself and remember only the case that supports your theory. I attained greater objectivity when I was working for a service for psychological personnel selection, about 1960. After lengthy interviews, I would note my predictions in the files of my most typical candidates; if my diagnosis were correct, they should preferably be born with Mars, Jupiter, Saturn or the Moon in one of the key sectors of the sky. After obtaining the birth hours of these subjects from the register offices, I found that my score of successful predictions was noticeably higher than my failures.

However, my sample was very small, and I had no real proof to convince other researchers that I had judged correctly and that planetary types applied to 'ordinary' people. What was required was a method enabling me to prove objectively that the planetary factors of personality, as described in relation to well-known people, could be found in everyone. The solution was obvious, particularly as I am a psychologist. I could use the modern tools for exploring personality, such as tests and questionnaires, to study the possible relations between planets and character traits. In fact, I had already carried out several experiments on the basis of a personality questionnaire.[15]

My first attempt was 20 years ago, when I put together a questionnaire of vocational interest much like Strong's, which is widely used in psychology, but considerably shorter and adapted to my observations.[16] It was based on the results obtained for Mars, Jupiter, Saturn and the Moon at the birth of well-known people, and was made up of 20 items (professions, activities, etc.) representing various interests. This questionnaire was published in 1966. Three examples of these items are given below: in each case, the subject was asked to circle one of the four activities he would prefer to be involved in, each of which was seen as having a link with either Mars, Jupiter, Saturn or the Moon; of course, the name of the planet 'corresponding' to each of these items was not given to the subject filling in the questionnaire.

sales representative (Jupiter)	engraver (Saturn)	gardener (Moon)	professional athlete (Mars)
chemist (Saturn)	poet (Moon)	surgeon (Mars)	actor (Jupiter)
to meet friends (Moon)	to collect stamps (Saturn)	to be a parade organizer (Jupiter)	to drive a sports car (Mars)

The questionnaire was completed by 300 subjects, mostly men, during psychological examinations held at the Société Française de Psychotechnique in Paris, between 1960 and 1961. The next stage was to obtain the date and hour of birth of each subject from the register offices in the places where they were born. Finally, the positions were calculated for Mars, Jupiter, Saturn and the Moon, in the 12 sectors of their daily movement.

My hypothesis was that subjects who preferred 'Mars answers' (professional athletes, surgeons, military men, etc.) should have been born more often with Mars in the key sectors of rise and culmination than the subjects making up the entire sample of 300 cases. And the same should apply for Jupiter, Saturn and the Moon with regard to items corresponding to other professional interests.

Unfortunately, my hypothesis was not confirmed by the results and, in fact, the experiment was a total failure: the 'Mars', 'Jupiter', 'Saturn' and 'Moon' subjects did not choose the type of activity or vocational interest which, according to our results with outstanding professional people, they should have found particularly attractive. Of course, the experiment was conducted before I had perfected my character trait method or established a description of the types of planetary personality. It was based entirely on the vocational interests which the subjects themselves declared to be theirs and was, I now realize, a fairly naive and excessively simplistic approach to the question. Psychologists have actually shown that the relationship between professional interest and psychobiological temperament is fairly weak. It is perfectly possible to be attracted to the theatre with an introverted temperament, or towards the sciences with an extroverted temperament; it is just that, in general, it makes it harder to succeed, as I had already shown.

In 1973, I made another attempt to study the relation between planet and character trait for 'ordinary' people. In an appendix to my book, *Cosmic Influences on Human Behaviour*, I included an experimental questionnaire under the heading 'What would your planetary type be?'.[17] It was built directly on the description of planetary factors of personality of well-known people according to their biographies, and consisted of 40 questions, ten each devoted to the planetary factors of Mars, Jupiter, Saturn and the Moon. For each question there were three possible responses – 'yes', 'yes or no' and 'no'. A tabulation sheet was provided for the reader, and he or she was requested to send in the date, hour and place of birth, as well as certain details about the manner of birth, together with the completed questionnaire. The example below shows a question corresponding to each planet:

You are aggressive and competitive (Mars)
You are considered witty in a sarcastic and bantering way
(Jupiter)
You seem modest and even shy (Saturn)
You tend to be naive and your whims are rather childish (Moon).

I received hundreds of replies from readers in different countries. During my stay in San Diego, I used the computer at Astro Computing Services to analyse the results, concentrating on questionnaires from an initial group of 846 subjects.

First of all, I studied the 'yes' answers, which are usually the most characteristic. In the hope of getting better results, I selected subjects who provided the clearest scores on the questionnaires – a high number of 'yes' answers to Mars questions, a high number of 'yes' answers to Jupiter questions, etc. As for my hypothesis, it was of course that the subjects born with a planet in one of the key sectors would answer 'yes' most often to those questions representative of the character traits linked with that planet.

The analysis of the results did not, unfortunately, confirm my hypothesis. The subjects who presented themselves as 'Mars', 'Jupiter', etc., types in their answers were not born more often than anybody else with Mars, Jupiter, etc., in the key sectors of the sky.

There could be several explanations for this renewed failure: the questionnaire may have been badly phrased, for instance, or the information about the hour of birth, supplied personally rather than by the register offices, may have been unreliable. But, after testing the questionnaire on several people I knew well, the most likely cause seemed to be that the subjects of the experiment were not capable of assessing themselves in answering the different questions asked.

If that were the case, would it not be easier simply to make use of some already established psychological questionnaire? A trial was made recently with the EPQ (Eysenck Personality Questionnaire) on a group of 561 subjects. The results were mildly positive, especially in terms of the Mars factor and extroversion and psychoticism.[18] But they are far from providing the clarity which we had every right to hope for, after the highly successful encounter between Eysenck's personality theory and ours, using the character traits taken from the biographies of outstanding people.

Better results could be obtained if the experiment with the EPQ were carried out more carefully. In our group of 561 subjects, the proportion of induced births was unknown, but was presumably considerable owing to the high proportion of births since 1950. Moreover, in the analysis of the results, I did not select the subjects who obtained the highest extreme scores at each of Eysenck's dimensions of personality. Hans Eysenck rightly suggests:

Given that there is already some evidence for a relationship between extroversion–introversion, or psychoticism, and planetary position, I think the optimum procedure would be to select subjects scoring high and low respectively on one or other of these personality dimensions, and then ascertain the planetary position at their birth, as well as whether their birth was natural or induced. This would reduce the numbers required drastically, and would at the same time enable one to conduct a much cleaner analysis of variance than by artificially dividing a random population in two.[19]

This suggestion is welcome. In the course of the experiment it might also be informative to ask outside observers familiar with the subject to fill up the EPQ on his behalf. Their assessments should validate the subject's own, since, according to Eysenck, 'there is almost 100 per cent agreement' between the two kinds of assessment and 'this is true particularly with extremes'. The results of this new EPQ experiment are eagerly awaited.

The problem is that none of the existing questionnaires has been worked out for the purpose of measuring planetary types. For instance, Cattell's 16PF is supposed to investigate 16 factors of the human personality, whereas I have only defined five planetary factors. Another major problem concerns the predictive value of most of these questionnaires. They may suffer from the same defects as mine, in that they ask people to assess themselves without appropriate outside controls. Is that reasonable? This raises the whole issue of self-evaluation as it relates to questionnaires, and needs to be considered in some depth.

However ingeniously a questionnaire is constructed, it is still essentially based on asking people with no psychological training whatever to assess themselves often in the most definitive manner. According to Professor Alan Smithers, of the department of education at the University of Manchester, it is very difficult to assess yourself properly. He has given a relevant analysis of the problem: 'The way personality has been measured depends on people describing themselves. The personality inventories and adjectival scales do not measure personality as such, but rather measure how people report themselves. How people report themselves will depend, among other things, on what they know about themselves, and presumably this knowledge will have been distilled from all the hints and clues received as life has been lived.'[20] This 'self-reporting nature of many psychological measures', to use Smithers's expression, is an extremely important factor and one which many researchers do not take into sufficient consideration. A belief in the quasi-infallibility of some well-known questionnaires as predictive tools for the human personality can induce errors, not only among professional psychologists, but also among scientists in other disciplines. And that sometimes happens in the field of astrology.

In their book *The Gemini Syndrome*, which takes a fairly hard line against astrology, the astronomers R. B. Culver and P. A. Ianna make a 'final offer' to astrologers: 'Given the times, dates and locations of birth of 30 individuals and the personality profile for these individuals as measured by an acceptable standardized test (such as the Minnesota Multiphasic Personality Inventory), match each horoscope with a personality profile to a level significantly better than chance ($p = 0.001$).'[21] What a challenge! Apparently, Culver and Ianna regard the MMPI with the utmost reverence, and their attitude seems highly surprising to a professional psychologist like myself. I have used the MMPI over several years in practice and, in my experience, the predictive value of this personality profile when based on the answers of *normal* people is more or less nil. (It is possible, although by no means sure, that the test may have greater value when applied to people with nervous disorders or psychoses, which is what it was initially designed to deal with.)

I would suggest that Culver and Ianna first make their 'final offer' to psychology rather than to astrology. They could ask psychologists to validate the psychological profiles of MMPI subjects by means of properly observed behaviour in the lives of these subjects, carefully controlled by a number of people.

It is a pity, too, that some astrologers appear to share with astronomers this naive belief in questionnaires such as Cattell's 16PF or the MMPI. Worse still, it has been shown that astrologers have occasionally fallen into a different trap – that of administering a questionnaire, in order to verify an astrological law, to subjects already acquainted with the law in question.[22] The result is that these subjects have a tendency 'to self-rate themselves in function of their personal horoscopes'.[23] I will return to this aspect in greater detail in chapter 7, where I discuss the attempts made by astrologers to justify the reality of the signs of the zodiac. Worst of all, I think, is to commit the double error of using a 'poor' questionnaire on an 'astrological' population.

Sometimes it is difficult to know how best to proceed. As far as I can see, a really effective method can be found by tackling the question from various different angles on a trial-and-error basis. However, I can suggest an approach which might give interesting results.[24]

Obviously, the ideal experimental conditions would enable one to work with ordinary people in exactly the same way as with outstanding figures. The aim would be to find some means of putting together biographical sketches of any individual and then to extract the character traits and behaviour contained in these potted biographies. Finally, one could apply the character-trait method, which worked so well before.

The main difficulty, of course, stems from the lack of biographical material. However, it might be possible to work out a standardized technique, which could be applied to all the cases one wished to analyse, using the subject's curriculum vitae, interviews and behaviour studies. The great problem, again, would be finding people to supply information about the subject and act as 'biographers' or 'psychologists'.

One could start by drawing up, for each subject, a short 'life history' based on objective, psychological criteria (profiles of activity, behaviour, achievements). This sort of 'case history' would make it possible to discern the character traits shown most consistently by the subject during his or her life. Members of the family and close friends would be asked to choose a certain number of traits to describe the subject's personality as precisely as possible, perhaps helped by a selection of traits taken from the type lists of planetary factors published by my laboratory (see the text published as the Appendix of this book). One would then keep only those traits on which there was a large consensus among the subject's 'judges'. Of course, psychologists could also be asked to reply on behalf of the subject after examining him or her at length. It goes without saying that these ideas would have to be tested first, before they could be accepted. And one can think of many other types of experiments.

It might be argued that 'personality inventories' have been devised in order to render unnecessary the use of the approach I advocate here. I think, however, that this approach is justified. Given that there is a lack of consistency among existing theories of personality, comparison of the results of the experiments I am suggesting and those of the personality inventories would be very informative. My other motive is more subjective, I confess. I would like to test myself. The use of personality description in ordinary language was such a fruitful idea, while we were dealing with outstanding people, that I am not ready to give it up now, in working with 'ordinary' people, without at least an attempt to use it.

I have recently come across an interesting work – *Personality Description in Ordinary Language* by D. B. Bromley, professor of psychology at the University of Liverpool – and was amazed to find, expressed in other terms, many of my own suggestions.[25] The book, we are told on the dust-jacket, is

about the way people describe each other in ordinary language in everyday life. It shows the connections between our common-sense understanding of others on the one hand and scientific or professional understanding on the other. This promising new approach to the scientific study of personality based on a non-quantitative, naturalistic method is capable of incorporating traditional clinical and psychometric approaches and offers an important contribution to the scientific study of individual cases.

Professor Bromley believes that, because of the increasingly obvious failure of some methods in the psychology of personality, we shall necessarily resort to what he calls the 'psychological case-study' or the 'psychological life study'. He explains: 'A psychological "case-study" is a scientific account, in ordinary language, of an individual person in normal or problematical circumstances. A psychological "life-study", by contrast, is a comprehensive account of the person's tendencies and characteristics revealed through an analysis of the principal episodes making up that person's life.' A little further on, he asserts: 'A psychological "case-study" provides us with an objective account of a real person as seen from the outside.' He gives an example: 'A person's "ambition" can be indicated by statements about his personality traits, his life history, his attitude to his family, his relationships with other people, his daily routine and his expressive behaviour.'

Professor Bromley shows how these ideas can be put into practice. He reports an experiment where he asked people to describe in a few lines the personality of a man or woman they liked or disliked. These brief portraits are highly instructive and give a good demonstration of the usefulness of this sort of evidence. My own 'neo-astrological' work will certainly benefit from contact with Professor Bromley's thinking.

I hasten to add that any convergence between us is limited to the interest we both have in 'personality description in ordinary language'. It implies no sort of belief on Professor Bromley's part in my theories, which he probably knows nothing about. Indeed, he expresses his scepticism about cosmic influence: 'Character is not determined by the position of the planets at one's time of birth.'[26]

In conclusion, I plan to test the possible correlation between planets and ordinary people in two different ways: by gathering personality extremes from the EPQ scores and by using again the personality descriptions given in ordinary language. Our knowledge of the subject is in fact poor. It will not be an easy process to create a really accurate methodology for ordinary people as efficient as that for well-known figures, and we must remember that the results will never be as spectacular. Celebrities tend to have strong personalities, and this is less often true of ordinary people. But it would be illogical to find no correlation at all between the personality of ordinary people and the position of the planets at their birth, especially as I have already observed a planetary effect on heredity among that very group.

I hope, too, that I have demonstrated how an appropriate method can rescue the research worker from the scepticism or disenchantment which a series of negative results might induce. I have learned from experience and have every confidence that the next experiment will be more conclusive.

Part Two

Neo-Astrology?

5

'Science' and Proof

Having started, in the beginning, from an unusual observation made during a study of astrology, I have come a long way during the past 30 years – to a psychological description of certain planetary types. It is time to step back and look at two fundamental questions. First of all, has science accepted my observations as authentic scientific fact? And secondly, to what extent can one see my results as confirming traditional astrology and the validity of horoscopes?

From the moment my first book came out in 1955, I had been scrupulous in describing my methods in detail and publishing all my sources, including the complete list of 6,000 births, with their hours, of the outstanding professional people on which I had been working.[1] With profound naivete, as I realize now, I had every expectation that interested scientists would talk of my work and criticize it – 'interested scientists' being, for me, those who had publicly declared their willingness to examine objectively the validity of any proofs of astral influence.

Paul Couderc, astronomer at the Paris Observatory, fitted that description. As early as 1951, he wrote: 'If the stars are an important factor in the personality of each individual, and played a part, *however small*, in the formation of bodily and spiritual characters, along with all the thousands of other factors which shape his destiny (heredity, environment, chance . . .) then it would be an incalculably valuable property. One could try and apply it for the good of mankind.'[2] According to Couderc, scientists were ready to examine any astrological law put before them and had formed various groups for that purpose, but 'unfortunately these commissions are short of work.'

Spurred by this challenge, I sent my book to a number of people, including those on the commissions of control and Paul Couderc himself. None of them replied, and I was to continue to bombard them for months, years even, until eventually I did get a reaction. But Couderc, between 1955 and his death at the end of 1980, remained completely silent. The fact that he occasionally pronounced on my works in public was my sole confirmation that he had ever received them. I shall return to this later.

The president of the American commission at this time was Bart J. Bok, later the guiding hand behind the notorious anti-astrological manifesto published in the *Humanist* in 1975, which I discussed at the beginning of this book. He wrote to me only once, in 1960, when I had sent him my second book.[3] His comment was: 'I should say that as of now I have neither the time nor the inclination to make further inquiries into astrology and its claims.'[4]

My initial experience with the committee of Belgian scientists, mentioned by Couderc, was no more encouraging. I had decided to concentrate all my efforts on them, particularly as they were much nearer than the American commission and there was no language barrier. Their full title was Le Comité Belge pour l'Investigation Scientifique des Phénomènes Réputés Paranormaux (The Belgian Committee for the Scientific Investigation of Phenomena said to be Paranormal – referred to here as the Para Committee), and the motto on their coat of arms read: 'Deny nothing *a priori*, assert nothing without proof.' Sylvain Arend, astronomer at the Royal Belgian Observatory, replied to my letter: 'Professional astronomers have studied the question *a priori*. For them, planets are nothing but celestial bodies which have cooled down and which do little more than reflect the radiation which they receive . . . . Moreover, it has become clear that human destinies are dependent on human factors and not on astral ones.'[5]

This latest reaction was particularly demoralizing: perhaps my work simply did not merit scientific control. Yet that was not the opinion of Jean Porte, statistician and administrator at the Institut National de la Statistique et des Etudes Econo-miques who, in 1956, analysed my results.[6] He began by criti-cizing my work, because he was hostile to the idea of astral influence. But he was objective and open to discussion, and never refused to exchange views about aspects of my method which he thought questionable. In the end, he accepted their validity and wrote in the preface to my volume on method in 1957: 'I have looked for errors in the present work – and I have found none.'[7] So, despite the attitude of Couderc, Bok and Arend, my work deserved to be examined and my experiments to be controlled.

In 1961, I made a fresh assault on the Belgian Para Com-mittee. Armed with Jean Porte's support, and encouraged by my new investigations into foreign births, I was determined this time to brook no refusal. The committee examined my methods and Jean Dath, professor of engineering at the Belgian Ecole Royale Militaire, wrote to me a year later: 'I have personally verified some of your results and I have not been able to find anything which, from a statistical point of view, is open to objec-tion.'[8] Verbally, however, he and other members of the com-mittee expressed themselves unconvinced by my results. It seemed to them that I had carried out the work correctly; but what if I had cheated or – more elegantly – what if I had made a more or less subconscious selection of the birth data to prove my thesis? I found this objection perfectly reasonable and pressed the committee to carry out another experiment with new data. The response was: 'We are unfortunately not able to do this, because the difficulties of getting together a new group of births are insurmountable.'

I had managed to penetrate the outer walls of 'Castle Para Committee', only to have the heavy doors of the keep slammed shut in my face. A strange phenomenon is never recognized by science unless independent researchers have rediscovered it by working through new data from beginning to end; and yet the committee refused to undertake that repetition.

Frustrated as I was, I welcomed the sympathy of other researchers engaged in studying aspects of the cosmos. Many of them were respected university professors, but were regarded with suspicion by their colleagues, whose conformist ideas they

were challenging in their various disciplines. In 1965, I met
Professor Piccardi, director of the physico-chemistry laboratory
at the University of Florence. For several years, he had been
struggling to achieve recognition for his work in cosmic chemistry, while rejecting any description of himself as an astrologer.
In Piccardi's view, there exist strict correlations between certain
cosmic phenomena, for instance sunspots, and the behaviour of
chemical reactions carried out under rigorously controlled laboratory conditions. His belief in a modification of chemical reactions by the cosmos was much less 'absurd' than the idea that
the rise of Mars is linked to the future sporting success of the
newborn child; and yet he enjoyed only a marginal status in
science. From our discussions together, Piccardi was convinced
that the 'Piccardi effect' and the 'Gauquelin effect' could make
common cause. In 1966, in a preface to one of my books, he
wrote: 'The facts which Gauquelin presents us with have been
controlled. . . . It is precisely because these well-*controlled* facts
do exist, that I can quite happily write this preface to Gauquelin's book, and try to relate the *Gauquelin facts* to other well-
known phenomena in order to promote a general revision of our
ideas with regard to modern scientific research.'[9]

The following year I met Frank A. Brown, professor of biology at Northwestern University, in Evanstown near Chicago.
Professor Brown was placed in a similar position in biology to
Piccardi's in chemistry. Innumerable experiments on plants and
animals had convinced him that living beings possess a 'biological clock' of great sensitivity, which can be constantly reset
by the movements of the heavenly bodies, the Sun and the
Moon in particular. The existence of a biological clock – or
rather, several biological clocks – in living beings was accepted
by other researchers. But what made Frank Brown's school
'suspect' was the fact that he attributed changes in biological
behaviour not solely to known physical factors such as light and
heat, but also to much more subtle influences linked to the
cosmos – infinitesimal variations in magnetic fields, for instance,
or the presence of extremely weak radiation or what are called
very long frequency waves. Thus Brown was in confrontation
with almost all the specialists who asserted the primacy of the
internal biological clock and maintained that it functioned in a
more or less autonomous way without the support of cosmic

influences. Having learned of my observations, he, like Piccardi, believed that the explanation might lie in a new way of thinking about relations between the cosmos and living beings. The 'Brown effect' and the 'Gauquelin effect' were similar and it might be possible to discover a common source for them both. He outlined his position in the preface to my book, published in 1967.[10]

With the support of Piccardi and Brown, I gradually managed to gain some sort of acceptance. My observations were presented at international scientific conferences, and I was even named a member of scientific societies like the International Society of Biometerology and the International Society of Chronobiology. But this apparent success was not enough to transform the 'Gauquelin effect' into a phenomenon recognized by science. Papers I gave at conferences were still received with scepticism, indifference, a 'variety of reactions', and attempts were made, often successfully, to remove my text from the published proceedings. What really worried me was the need for other researchers to undertake my experiments on new material, independently of me. I had repeated my experiments scores of times, but that was not enough, even for my own satisfaction.

I decided to approach the Brussels Para Committee once again. Five years had elapsed since our last contact, and I thought I had found a way of overcoming the 'insurmountable' difficulty of collecting unpublished data on another group of births of outstanding people. The solution was to work on sports champions. Sporting glory is swift but ephemeral, and hundreds of sportsmen had risen to prominence in the 12 years since I had published my initial results. I was helped in my project by Professor Luc de Marré of Antwerp, a member of the committee who was not too violently hostile to my ideas.

The committee agreed to set up an original experiment on a new group of French and Belgians, with the help of a data-processing machine, and we settled the details about procedure and results. If I were to be vindicated, the investigation would have to show that champions were born more often after the rise and culmination of Mars than non-champions. I took precautions to prevent any doubt about the final outcome of the experiment and whether it was a success or failure; and I made sure that no one, myself included, would be able to shelter

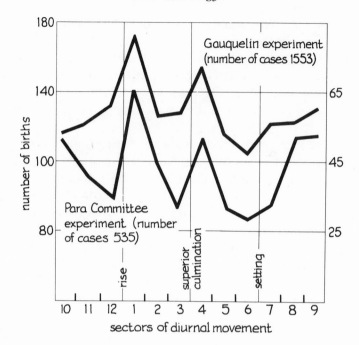

Figure 21   The Mars effect and sports champions: comparison of
Gauquelin and Para Committee results
Sources: M. Gauquelin, *Les Hommes et les Astres* (1960); and in *Journal of
Interdisciplinary Cycle Research* 3 (1972); and Para Committee in *Nouvelles
Brèves* 43 (1976)

behind some later reinterpretation of the results. On 4 March
1967 I wrote to the president of the committee, Professor
Koenigsfeld of Liège: 'In order for the new experiment to verify
our earlier work, the group studied must present a surplus of the
position of Mars after the rise and culmination.'[11] On 22
October 1968, the committee sent me the results as they had
come out of the computer. The new findings relating to the
births of 535 champions confirmed my earlier observations with
complete clarity on the statistical level, as can be seen in figure
21.

I expected that the committee would now recognize the validity of my conclusions and immediately publish the results, but
nothing happened. Jean Dath, professor of engineering at the
Ecole Royale Militaire, and Jean Dommanget, astronomer at the
Brussels Royal Observatory, who had worked actively on the

project, instead began to doubt my methods, although they had accepted them six years earlier. A discussion then ensued on the value of the calculation of theoretical frequencies, which would, according to the committee, reveal a fault to explain the 'Mars effect' by some 'normal' cause. A highly technical dossier grew up over the years. The committee undertook counter-experiments which all turned out in my favour, and it even questioned the use of classic statistical formulae. The results stood up to it all: by 1972, the facts remained, first, that the committee had observed the same 'abnormal' results as I had and, secondly, that it had not been able to find fault in my method and the results could only be explained in terms of a correlation between the planet Mars and the births of sports champions. Yet the members of the Para Committee still did not publish anything, maintaining that they had found an error in my method which would explain everything. Professor Remy Chauvin, director of the laboratory of animal sociology at the Sorbonne, quotes in one of his books the reply he had received from Professor Koenigsfeld: 'We have, in fact, verified M. Gauquelin's calculations and we are in agreement with them. . . . But what we are not in agreement about are his conclusions, which we cannot accept.'[12]

My relations with the Para Committee were deteriorating. I took the initiative and presented the committee's results myself at a scientific conference, to the annoyance of the committee members.[13] Nevertheless, Dommanget and Dath decided to put in hand the long-deferred account of their experiment.[14] The main conclusion of the report was that a simple demographic law lay behind the so-called 'Mars effect', which is why sports champions were born more often when Mars was on the rise. However, no numerical proof was offered for their assertion. This is the account given by Professor Luc de Marré, a former member of the committee who had been heavily 'involved in the work of the Belgian Para Committee regarding the so-called Mars effect':

> As a matter of fact, the committee was unable to discover any mistake or error in Mr Gauquelin's calculations or in the results which he claimed. . . . The results of these counter-experiments tended to confirm Mr Gauquelin's hypothesis. In particular, a

sliding of the birth hours, in function of the alphabetical order of
the champions, showed beyond all dispute that Gauquelin's theoretical (expected) frequencies were correct. In September 1976
the committee published a 17-page report on its work concerning
the research. It was astonishing to see that it did *not* mention any
of these counter-experiments; on the contrary, it accused Mr
Gauquelin of imaginary demographic errors. This latter item was
the more surprising as it was Mr Gauquelin himself who had
informed Mr Dommanget, a member of the committee, about the
existence of a demographic problem which had to be solved, as
well as about the means to achieve that solution.[15]

The astronomer Paul Couderc, whom I mentioned earlier,
apparently altered his opinions. In 1967, 11 years after the publication of my first book, he was still stating publicly: 'M. Gauquelin's results are without value, his methods are confused, and
no scientist worthy of the name would accept them.'[16] But, in
1974, his tone changed, and an entirely revised edition of his
book, *l'Astrologie,* appeared. In it the author devoted a 14-page
chapter to my work, under the intentionally enigmatic heading
'The case of M.G.'. To my surprise, he recognized me (at least
the M.G. in question) as 'a sincere, learned and extremely active
researcher'; he 'admired the wealth of publications put out by
my laboratory'; and he mentioned the verification of the Mars
effect by the Para Committee.[17]

Then, in 1978, a new edition of the book came out. Meanwhile, the Para Committee report, describing my supposed
errors of method, had been published. Couderc now told his
readers: 'M.G. has certainly underestimated the complexity of
astronomical questions which he thought to represent accurately
in elementary formulae. The astronomers and statisticians of the
Para Committee, after a conscientious examination, have
declared these formulae to be inadequate. This conclusion will
reassure all those whom M.G.'s propositions have alarmed.'[18] I
wonder whether that conclusion reassured Couderc himself,
especially as he knew – having been told by his colleague, Jean
Porte, as early as 1957 – that the Mars effect could not be
explained by any error on my part.[19]

In 1975 Hans Eysenck, the famous and controversial professor
of psychology at the University of London, wrote: 'I think it

may be said that, as far as objectivity of observation, statistical significance of differences, verification of the hypothesis, and replicability are concerned, there are few sets of data in psychology which could compete with these observations. Full details of all the persons included in these studies are given in the voluminous publications of the Gauquelins, and I have checked a small random sample of easily accessible ones. . . I think we must admit that there is something here that requires explanation.'[20] This was to lead to the fruitful collaboration described in chapter 4.

It might be said that psychologists do not suffer from the same prejudices as astronomers; but that was not my own experience. In 1976, the XXI International Congress of Psychology was held in Paris, with Paul Fraisse, director of the institute of psychology at the University of Paris, as president and Professor Jean-François Le Ny heading the scientific committee. I intended to present a paper to the congress, together with Eysenck, and took the precaution of contacting members of the scientific committee and submitting data from my laboratory as well as reprints of articles published abroad. The paper was refused 'by the unanimous decision of the members of the scientific committee', according to Le Ny, because 'it seemed to the committee that there is lacking the information necessary for assessing the criteria on which you based your sample of persons studied.'[21] So, although I am a professional psychologist, I was unable to participate in the international congress of psychology organized in my own country in 1976. I attended others certainly, but abroad.[22]

With the Para Committee refusing to recognize the evidence, the situation seemed to have reached stalemate. In 1975, however, the anti-astrological manifesto signed by 192 'leading scientists' was published in the American journal, the *Humanist* (see Prelude). It was accompanied by an article by Lawrence J. Jerome, a 'scientific writer', who rejected my work as totally valueless and claimed that I had made monumental mistakes.[23] With all the publicity surrounding the manifesto, the article brought my name to the notice of people in America and elsewhere, even if not in a particularly favourable light. And

Jerome's criticisms were so far-fetched that I had no trouble dealing with them in the next issue of the *Humanist*, citing, of course, the Para Committee's repetition of the Mars effect among sports champions. The editor, Paul Kurtz, then wrote to members of the committee for their opinion; they, while voicing their 'demographic' criticisms, admitted that they had observed the same Mars effect as I had. I replied in my turn that demography did not enter into it as far as the effect was concerned.

Kurtz now sought the advice of Marvin Zelen, professor of statistical sciences at the University of Harvard. He confirmed that Jerome's mathematical arguments were insignificant but, being neither demographer nor astronomer, was unable to evaluate the justice of the Para Committee's objection. Instead, he proposed an experiment which, in his view, could prove whether the Mars effect existed or not.[24] If it is true, said Zelen, that the Mars effect at the birth of champions is nothing but the consequence of a demographic law, then all non-champions born on the same day and in the same place as the champions ought to demonstrate the same Mars effect – that is, ought to have been born in greater numbers at the rise and culmination of the planet. All that was necessary was to write to the register offices of the places where the champions were born, requesting the hours of birth of everyone born on the same day of the same year as they were and thus under identical astronomical and demographic conditions. Calculation of the position of Mars at the hour of these births would provide the desired answer.

I agreed to the 'Zelen test' and managed to assemble, with the help of Professor Luc de Marré in Belgium, over 16,000 birth hours of non-champions born the same week and in the same place as the champions. According to our agreement, I sent Paul Kurtz photocopies of all the birth data obtained from the register offices. The results of the 'Zelen test' were published in the *Humanist* in 1977.[25] They show clearly that non-champions, born under the same conditions as champions, do not display the Mars effect, and that this effect can be observed only among the champions.

But victory was illusory. An article appeared, signed jointly by Paul Kurtz, editor of the *Humanist*, George Abell, astronomer at the University of California, Los Angeles, and by Marvin Zelen himself.[26] In it, the authors transform the test on non-champions into a test on champions and then, after the event, reduce the experiment to fragments, after eliminating the test-group of female champions (which, coincidentally, gave the result most favourable to me). Having diminished the value of the test in this way, they conclude: 'What shall we believe? If one had a high prior "belief" that there is a Mars effect, then the Gauquelin data would serve to confirm this prior belief. On the other hand, if the prior belief in the existence of the Mars effect was low, then this data may raise the posterior belief, but not enough to accept the existence of the Mars effect.'[27] The article ends with a query about my honesty in gathering the test data.

The reaction was varied: some were reassured by this defence of the established order in science; others, looking at the real results of the test, were disturbed. Elisabeth L. Scott, for instance, professor of statistics at the University of California, Berkeley, had signed the anti-astrological manifesto in 1975 and, like Zelen, Kurtz and Abell, was a member of the commission of control on the Mars effect. She wrote to them: 'Dr Gauquelin visited Berkeley last week and we had several interesting discussions. One concerned your recent article published in the *Humanist*. You sent me a pre-print of this paper and I telephoned each of you because I feel strongly that the discussion may be misleading. I understand that the paper was published virtually unchanged. What I would like to do now is to publish a short note, or even a letter, stating clearly what I think your error is. Is this a possibility? Would you publish such a note?'[28] For one reason or another, the note never appeared.

Henry Krips, professor at the department of history and philosophy of science at Melbourne University, produced a thorough analysis, largely devoted to my work and the commentaries on the Zelen test. He considered the conclusions drawn by Zelen, Kurtz and Abell to be hardly fair and, indeed, rather clumsy.[29] And a Canadian researcher, Eric Tarkington, maintained: 'There can be no doubt: the existence of the Mars effect has been demonstrated beyond all reasonable reservations. . . . The response of the *Humanist* represented a combination of shock and high comedy not likely to be repeated for a long time to come.'[30] As he demonstrates, 'The Committee says that the proportion of Mars in key sectors for the general population is

the same as the proportion among athletes; much to the contrary: the data shows that the chance of this being true is a good
deal less than one in a million.'[31]

In 1976, Paul Kurtz announced the creation of a 'Committee for
the Scientific Investigation of Claims of the Paranormal'
(CSICOP), of which he would be co-chairman. Both its title and
objectives were very similar to those of the Belgian Para Committee, and one of its first projects was to collect dates and hours
of birth of sports champions born in the USA, in order to test
the Mars effect again. Kurtz did not consult me in advance
about precise formulae for the experiments, but in August 1978,
passing through Paris, he showed me the results. I noted with
satisfaction that the Mars effect was clearly visible among the
most well-known sportsmen in the group (Olympic champions,
etc.) and that it disappeared among sportsmen who had not
reached the same level of celebrity. The results of the American
test agreed perfectly with my own observations, that planetary
effects are observable only if a certain degree of fame has been
achieved.[32]

Yet, according to Kurtz, Zelen and Abell, the American test
showed the absence of any Mars effect. They claimed that *all*
the sportsmen in the test were 'famous champions' and that the
Mars effect should therefore have been visible over the whole
group of births assembled by Kurtz, if the results were to confirm my thesis.[33] I opposed this interpretation and demonstrated, with the help of objective criteria measuring celebrity,
that the Mars effect was the more marked the more famous
Kurtz's sportsmen were.[34]

The argument which followed and was waged in the pages of
the *Skeptical Inquirer* had, in fact, been brewing between Kurtz,
Zelen, Abell and myself for over a year. At the end of 1978, I
wrote to Kurtz substantially as follows: 'It is clear that the
famous American champions show the Mars effect. But it is also
true that their number is too small to be really significant, as a
result of the administrative difficulties which you encountered
in gathering your data in the USA.' I then revived the idea,
proposed by Zelen himself, of increasing the number of famous
sportsmen, by including European champions who had arrived

on the international scene too recently to feature in the previous investigations. I suggested that Kurtz himself should draw up a list of the most famous champions among the 3,000 names in the *Dictionnaire des Sports*, an enormous encyclopaedic work which had just been published.[35] Kurtz did not reply. Even after I had visited him personally in the USA in the spring of 1979, as well as Abell and Zelen, there was no interest in my proposal. So I decided to undertake the experiment myself and managed to find out the hour of birth of 435 new sports champions born in five European countries. Once more, the Mars effect showed itself, strikingly.[36]

At this stage, Kurtz expressed his disagreement along these lines, which strongly suggest that my sample taken from the *Dictionnaire des Sports* is biased: 'Interestingly, in Gauquelin's new study the names of 423 famous sports champions who appear in (the) dictionary of sport are explicitly excluded as being "less renowned".'[37] To meet his accusation, I sent Kurtz the huge *Dictionnaire des Sports* and wrote suggesting that he himself draw up the complete list of *all* the sportsmen cited in the book.[38] I could predict that, without any selection whatsoever, the Mars effect would remain clearly visible. A year later, despite regular correspondence from me, Kurtz refused the offer.[39]

In October 1981, a bombshell exploded, in the form of an article entitled 'sTarbaby', by Dennis Rawlins.[40] A violent attack on the attitude of CSICOP throughout the Mars effect affair, it opens: 'They call themselves the Committee for the Scientific Investigation of Claims of the Paranormal. In fact, they are a group of would-be debunkers who bungled their major investigation, falsified the results, covered up their error and gave the boot to a colleague who threatened to tell the truth.' Rawlins himself was the colleague, an astronomer who has never made any secret of his scepticism about so-called 'paranormal' phenomena. He was one of the most active founders of CSICOP and on the executive council from 1976 to 1979. This explains the devastating force of 'sTarbaby', for the criticism of the way CSICOP had behaved came from within the organization itself.

In his article, Rawlins accused CSICOP – and its chairman, Paul Kurtz, in particular – of intellectual dishonesty for refusing to recognize that the Zelen test had confirmed my findings. Rawlins had asked Kurtz, Zelen and Abell to adopt a more objective and realistic attitude; as early as 1977, he had produced a memorandum demonstrating that the Zelen test could only support me and dismissing the imputation of imaginary errors by the Belgian Para Committee. In his view, the position of the Para Committee was nothing but an 'alibi': 'Gauquelin had made fair allowance of the effect under investigation.'[41] There was no response from Kurtz, Zelen and Abell.[42]

In 'sTarbaby' Rawlins also queried the manner in which Paul Kurtz conducted the test on American sports champions. He was well placed to do so, since Kurtz had asked him to draw up the astronomical calculations for Mars and the theoretical frequencies. The other members of CSICOP apparently played no part, and Rawlins did everything except gather the birth data, which Kurtz did alone without reference to Zelen and Abell. My own analysis of the structure of the data had pinpointed anomalies in this particular area, casting doubt on its objectivity. But Kurtz had assembled the sample on his own presumably, according to Rawlins, because he wished to maintain personal control over the data and results; otherwise, why should Kurtz have sent him 'the first set of data secretly, saying that he wished a private advance look at how the computation was going to come out'?[43]

Another sentence in Rawlins's article is revealing: 'At one point (after 120 names), I told Kurtz by phone that the key-sector score was now 22 per cent. He groaned.'[44] One can understand the reason: that was precisely the percentage of Mars in the 'key sectors' (sectors of rise and culmination) which should be observed, to confirm the existence of the Mars effect in champions. Curiously, the birth data of American athletes collected by Kurtz after these first 120 names give a percentage of Mars in the key sectors so small as to constitute an 'anti-Mars effect', especially for all the names at the end. Rawlins writes: 'No sooner was this task finished and the American test supposedly completed than Kurtz phoned me up and said oops, we accidentally missed a lot of names. . . . I returned to San Diego some weeks later. The last 82 names came in at summer's end.'[45]

It was in this group of 82 cases, which Kurtz had 'forgotten', that the Mars effect was only 7 per cent, as opposed to the 22 per cent observed among the names of the first 120 champions. In a letter to Kurtz at the end of 1978, I asked him to explain this sudden drop in percentages, but he did not reply.[46]

Rawlins and his 'sTarbaby' caused quite a stir in the scientific world. Some leapt to the defence of Kurtz and CSICOP; others expressed their disgust at the methods used in the name of science, and there were even resignations from CSICOP.[47] R. A. MacConnell, research professor of biophysics at the University of Pittsburg, circulated a letter to all the fellows and scientific consultants of CSICOP: 'On the basis of personal knowledge gained directly from present and past members of the executive council of the committee, I am convinced that Rawlins's report is certainly true in broad outline and probably true in every detail. Rawlins's "total recall" leaves little to the imagination. He has created a document of importance for the history of philosophy of science. . . . One scientist has summarized it in this way: Rawlins has uncovered the biggest scandal in the history of rationalism.'[48]

Of course, Rawlins himself has come under attack. Yet none of the members of CSICOP have been able to give satisfactory public replies to the specific accusations made in 'sTarbaby'. And the controversy still rages even as I write.[49]

One of those who resigned at an early stage from CSICOP – before the argument about the Mars effect developed – was Professor Marcello Truzzi, of the department of sociology at Eastern Michigan University.[50] He was originally named co-chairman with Paul Kurtz, but soon left the committee to set up his own journal, the *Zetetic Scholar*, 'an independent scientific review of claims of anomalies and the paranormal'. It is a remarkable publication which encourages dialogue, at a very high level, in various subjects such as UFOs, parapsychology, astrology. Truzzi has also founded the Center for Scientific Anomalies Research (CSAR), with himself as director and a group of researchers, most of them university professors.

While he was still co-chairman of CSICOP, Truzzi had witnessed the first skirmishes over the Mars effect and he later

decided to air the problem in the pages of his journal. He com-
missioned Patrick Curry, a young English philosopher of science
interested in astrology, whose investigation was published in
1982.[51] Curry covers the same ground as Rawlins in 'Tarbaby'.
However, he had completed the work by the end of July 1981,
before the publication of Rawlins's article, so was not influenced
by Rawlins and, in addition, had no axe to grind. As Truzzi
writes in his introduction: 'Readers of Rawlins' article will find
Curry's analysis comparatively dispassionate and more interested in issues of method than those of motives. Curry's charges
are therefore more serious.'[52] Curry's article is a very full document, a true lawyer's brief, and rests entirely on citing existing
texts (articles, letters, etc.). He concludes by denouncing
CSICOP's unscientific attitude throughout the affair:

> I don't think I need to stress how badly the committee has
> handled the investigation of the Mars effect; the facts above
> speak for themselves. Their work could now best function as a
> model and a warning of how *not* to conduct such an investigation.
> Given the ample internal (Rawlins) and external (Gauquelin)
> warnings that went suppressed or ignored, it is even difficult to
> accept protestations of 'good faith' and 'naivete' (Abell). Rawlins
> and Gauquelin are in fact the only two major figures to emerge
> with scientific credibility intact. It seems to me that this situation
> must call into question any further (unrefereed, at least) CSICOP
> involvement in research on the Mars effect, and possible other
> 'paranormal' areas.[53]

Six months before publication of Curry's article in the *Zetetic
Scholar*, Marcello Truzzi sent advance copies of the text to the
principal protagonists, including Kurtz, Zelen and Abell. There
was no response. (I am pleased to add at proof stage that in the
Spring 1983 issue of *Skeptical Inquirer* they acknowledge some of
their errors.)

Returning to my own country, in 1979 the 'Comité Français
pour l'Etude des Phénomènes Paranormaux' (CFEPP) was
founded, with the same avowed aims as its big brothers, the Para
Committee of Belgium and CSICOP. Its president in that year
was Jean-Claude Pecker, astrophysicist, professor at the Collège
de France, and member of the Academy of Sciences. I have

already illustrated Pecker's fundamental mistrust of astrology (see Prelude), and he has publicly criticized my own works, using Lawrence Jerome's and the Para Committee's arguments.[54] As he himself admitted, he had only 'second-hand knowledge', and yet he refused to meet me. A letter to me in 1975 ends: 'I ask you not to send me your publications any more, and you may consider it entirely useless to write to me.'[55]

Given this background, it might seem strange that, in 1982, CFEPP has expressed a wish to verify the Mars effect. The reason can be traced to an article by their secretary general, Michel Rouzé, a scientific journalist – unwittingly playing a similar role to Jerome with his unfortunate article in the *Humanist* in 1975, which forced Kurtz to verify the Mars effect. Rouzé's piece appeared in *Science et Vie*, a French journal with a wide circulation, in 1981, and announced that CSICOP had finally demolished the Mars effect: 'This time the facts seem definite: sportsmen no more have Mars than Neptune at the ascendant.'[56] Rouzé brought Rawlins into the debate, as 'this disinterested judge' who had finally come down on the side of Kurtz, Zelen and Abell against the Mars effect – Rawlins was actually in the process of writing his vitriolic 'sTarbaby'. Rouzé also cast doubt on my scientific integrity: the Mars effect was due to a 'doubtful manipulation of statistics' and to my 'skill in fitting up graphs'. Referring to the Zelen test, he espoused the theories put forward by CSICOP; and describing the test made in Belgium, he made use of the Para Committee's alibis.

As a regular contributor to *Science et Vie,* I knew the editor, Philippe Cousin, and asked for the right of reply. This was refused but, when I persisted, Cousin came up with a counter-proposal: 'I am a member of CFEPP like Rouzé and, if you like, I will ask the members of CFEPP to undertake a fresh verification of the Mars effect. The results will be published in *Science et Vie.* Do you agree to accept this as compensation?'[57] I did, of course, agree. To make sure that the same mishap did not occur as with CSICOP, I immediately drew up an extremely precise, six-page statement of terms for the experiment, and sent this to CFEPP by registered post in April 1981.[58]

This explains how the members of CFEPP were prepared to verify the Mars effect – apparently, at least, for nothing has yet been done as I write these lines in April 1982. In January 1982, I managed to arrange a meeting with Professors Galifret and

Schatzman (both members of CSICOP), Philippe Cousin and Michel Rouzé himself. It is largely on him that will fall the crucial task of controlling the experiment and, although I have asked for 'neutral' observers at the French test, this has been rejected.[59]

All this expenditure of energy and flood of words to defend the Mars effect – an effect which represents less than five per cent of the numerous observations I have published over more than a quarter of a century. My opponents are a generation behind me. But you cannot always choose the field of battle on which to defend your ideas and work. And that the field of battle should be Mars – what a symbol for astrology! It won't be the first time that the planet has featured in a scientific revolution: in struggling to understand the activity of Mars, which refused to behave according to Ptolemy's classic theory of epicycles, Kepler, the astrologer-astronomer, discovered the true laws of the movement of the planets. He revived a stagnant medieval astronomy to lay the foundations of the modern science. I like to think that again it will be thanks to Mars, the rebel planet against 'official' scientists, that astrology – as stultified today as once astronomy was – will become a science, a caterpillar at last transformed into a butterfly.

I hope the reader will forgive me for having sung the odyssey of a certain Michel Gauquelin, 25 years in the grip of what Thomas S. Kuhn calls 'normal science'.[60] I believe that this tale has value beyond the question of myself and my discoveries, as an example in the philosophy and sociology of science.[61] But it would be complacent to think that the voyage is over: other 'scientific' committees, other controls lie in wait, and that is just as well. I must never forget that the influence of the planets, even reduced to the modest proportions I have assigned it, remains a provocation for the average scientist today. He has the duty to be sceptical and even, perhaps, the right to be slightly unjust. The rationalist is disarmed by the apparent absurdity of things: he must fight this 'absurdity' blindly, or he must flee it; either way, he is sure to be right. And yet, as Bertrand Russell has written: 'Not to be absolutely certain is, I think, one of the essential things about rationality.'

6

The Triumph of the
Astrological Idea

Some years ago, I spoke at a meeting organized by the Rationalist Union of Paris on the theme, 'Why astrologers?' (with the
implication, 'Why so many charlatans and credulous fools?').
The president of the session, Professor Yves Galifret, secretary
general of the Rationalist Union, listened until I had finished
and then said: 'What bothers me most in your account, you see,
is that it should be the planet Mars which governs champions,
and not some other planet. I would much have preferred
Venus.' The irony of the remark masked a genuine discomfort.
According to traditional astrology, Mars is the god of war, the
red planet, influencing battles and conferring qualities such as
courage and aggressiveness. To scientists, a first 'absurdity' is
that there should be a relationship between a planet at birth and
professional destiny; but a second, more deep-seated than the
first, is any agreement between the symbolism of the planet and
the personality of the individual. Yet there is no avoiding the
question that everyone wants to ask: what kind of light do my
planetary effects throw on the reality of astrology? Is the example of Mars just a coincidence, which astrologers can turn to
their advantage?

Before investigating the matter, a word of caution. There are
those who see in my work new proof of the validity of the
horoscope, as against those who regard it as an illusory demonstration of limited interest. The conflict is between two ways of
thinking, each equally conformist – 'horoscopism' versus 'scient-
ism'. The latter, as we have seen, is defended by a sort of

'official' science, although this must be distinguished from the scientific community as a whole; the former belongs to the world of professional astrologers, who have a different academism of their own, that of the horoscope. We must remain fully aware of the reality of facts and be careful not to fall into the trap of either extreme.

In astrology's favour, my work has demonstrated its fundamental assumption – the role played by astral influences at the moment of birth. Moreover, the planetary effect on personality is compatible with a certain diagnostic application. On the basis of the natal position of a planet in relation to the horizon and the meridian, it is possible to establish a prognostication of the future temperament and behaviour of the newborn child. Astrologers claim no more, except that their claims extend much further than anything I have been able to prove. I have only observed a correlation linked to certain planets and under certain astronomical conditions, namely their place in the diurnal movement; and the effects I have noted are only statistical laws. This is why I believe that planetary effects must always be considered along with the role played by hereditary factors, education, social position and chance in the make-up of the individual. Some modern astrologers share this point of view, I must say.

So, I have not confirmed the horoscope, but simply the effect of some planets during the course of their diurnal movement. This astronomical factor corresponds to the 'houses' of astrological doctrine. Every day, on account of the rotation of the Earth, the planets go through 12 houses. When the planet rises, it has just left House I and is entering House XII and, in the course of 24 hours, it progresses regularly across the sky, passing through the 12 houses in reverse order of their numbers. Contrary to the logic of astronomy, the houses are numbered backwards.

How, then, does the astrological meaning of the 12 houses compare with the laws of planetary intensity, as recorded during their diurnal movement? Are there points of contact between the horoscope and my observations, which might confirm the interpretations made by astrologers?

First of all, it must be acknowledged that for most astrologers the horizon-meridian axis is vitally important. They attribute a particular role and significance to the four 'angles' of the heavens – the Ascendant, Midheaven, Descendant, and IC (Immun Coeli, literally Lower Heaven) – as well as to the planets found in them. This is a long-standing tradition going back to Greek and Roman astrologers and the writings of Ptolemy and Manilius.[1] A planet rises when it is in the Ascendant, travels towards its superior culmination at the Midheaven, sets at the Descendant and goes through its inferior culmination at the Lower Heaven. In orthodox astrology, as described by Margaret Hone, a leading modern astrologer: 'The strength of Angularity is better expressed by saying that planets are undoubtedly strong when they are close to one of the angles, especially to the Ascendant or Midheaven, irrespective of which side of these they may be.'[2]

However, each planet automatically finds itself in one of the 12 astrological houses of the horoscope, and here things seem less happy for the cause of astrology. Figure 22 illustrates the discrepancy between astrological belief and my own findings. Figure 22a represents, according to astrology, the intensity of a planet going through the 12 houses in 24 hours; figure 22c shows, according to my observations, the zones of high intensity of a planet during the course of its daily movement. Comparing the two, it is obvious that the two laws of intensity only overlap on a narrow band just around the horizon-meridian axis. Moreover, as far as my work has demonstrated, the zones of maximum influence for a planet are situated almost entirely *after* the horizon and the meridian, roughly equivalent to Houses XII, IX, VI and III. Yet astrological tradition calls these regions of the sky 'cadent houses' (from the Latin *cadere*, to fall) and maintains that the planets in these houses can only have a weak and sometimes harmful influence. Thus Margaret Hone gives as 'keywords' for these cadent houses 'dispersion of ideas and energies'.[3]

On the other hand, the 'angular houses', I, IV, VII and X, situated *before* the horizon-meridian axis, are supposed to confer maximum potency on the planets within them. This Margaret Hone expresses in the keywords 'powerful; initiatory'.[4] The famous astrologer, Paul Choisnard, describes this fundamental

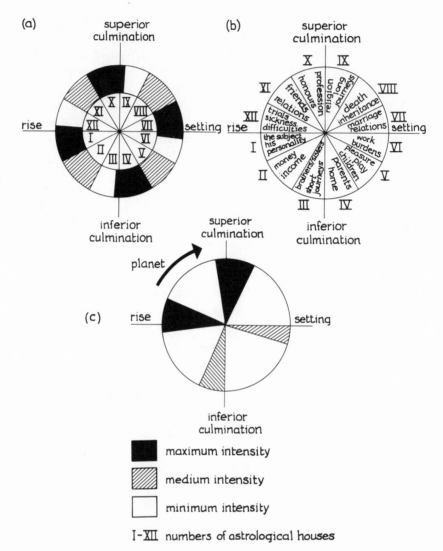

Figure 22 Intensity and meaning of the planet in the course of its diurnal movement according to astrology (top) and our observations (bottom)

law as follows: 'They are, in brief, the areas of the sky where the planets find themselves *on the point* of crossing the meridian or the horizon. And one can well imagine that an influence which is *growing* impresses a more powerful orientation on the newborn child than an influence which is *waning*.'[5] Unfortunately, statistical evidence runs counter to this reasoning.

As well as intensity, the 12 houses all have their own meaning, which is highly significant in astrological interpretation. Each house is concerned with one particular department of human life (see figure 22b), and this is crucial to the horoscope since, depending on the house it is in, the planet is seen as governing that department. However, the aspects of destiny ruled by each of the cadent houses, which are in my zones of greatest intensity, have nothing in common with my own observations.

House XII (just after the rise), is 'the hell of the zodiac',[6] connected with hidden enemies, prisons, ambushes, sickness and misfortunes of every kind; 'retirement; escape; sacrifice; hidden life of the unconscious' are the keywords used by Margaret Hone to define the influence of this house.[7] House IX (just after the superior culmination) is related to long journeys, religion, philosophy and large animals; or, in the words of Margaret Hone 'longer communications; more profound mental interests'. House VI (just after the setting) is concerned with health and its tribulations, acute illness in particular, as well as work difficulties. House III (just after the inferior culmination) is associated with immediate contacts, brothers and sisters, short journeys and small animals.

None of this agrees with the interpretation of my results. The contradiction between the unhealthy influence of House XII, that of the rising planet, and the considerable number of well-known people born with the planet in this zone of the sky is only too obvious. And what relevance have large animals, religion and philosophy for all those who succeed with a planet in House IX, immediately after the superior culmination?

To give a more concrete example of the conflicting evidence, House I, situated *before* the rise, is the house of character in astrology. It is, moreover, an angular house and therefore has special importance. Yet we find that the dynamic planet Mars is less often in House I at the birth of 'strong-willed' champions than it is for 'weak-willed' champions. At the same time, 'strong-willed' champions tend to come into the world later, after the rise of Mars, when the planet finds itself in the evil House XII, the house of ambushes and all sorts of difficulties.

House X, situated *before* the superior culmination, is the part of the sky reserved by astrologers for professional success and is also an angular house. Since my work has been concerned with professional achievement – in the shape of well-known scientists, famous painters, and so on – it is naturally of great interest. But it emerges that the taciturn and scientific planet Saturn, for instance, is *much less frequent* in House X at the birth of scientists than it is for artists, which goes against astrological tradition. And it is afterwards that the births of scientists increase, when Saturn is in House IX – the house of long journeys and large animals, a cadent house in fact, where there is 'dispersion of ideas and energies'.

There would seem to be only one conclusion. In linking the diurnal movement of the planets to the domain of astral influences and in emphasizing the role of the horizon-meridian axis, astrology has certainly come close to the truth. But, under the traditional form employed by the practitioner for diagnoses and predictions, the division of the diurnal movement into houses inevitably leads to major errors. Alternatively, my own observations are wrong. Whatever the case may be, the discrepancy between my laws of planetary intensity and the rules of astrology is very marked. Perhaps a more attentive historian of astrology could one day find out the reasons for this gulf: it might be that the ancients knew precisely where to place the zones of high and weak planetary intensity and, indeed, some contemporary astrologers are convinced that this is so. Nevertheless, astrology continues to apply laws which are apparently formulated in the opposite direction to mine, despite the fact that my work has been widely available for the past 25 years.

Astrology may find a ray of hope in the area of planetary symbolism, probably the most ancient of all astrological systems. In rudimentary form, it can be traced back to the Chaldeans some 4,000 years ago. It would seem that the code for each planet, or its symbolism, was based quite simply on its appearance. The brilliant Venus was the seat of Ishtar, goddess of fertility; ruddy Mars, the dwelling of the god of war, Negal; Jupiter, with its regular and lordly bearing, belonged to Marduk, king of the gods, powerful and terrible; finally Saturn, yellow and tremulous, was the home of Ninib, personified as a bad-tempered old man. 'The name Mars was given to a rock, and then afterwards it was seen as being a factor in war and as conferring a *martial* character on its subject,' declared the astronomer,[8] who saw nothing in this reasoning but a fine example of primitive mentality. The wonder lies in the discovery that people born at the rise or culmination of Mars really do have a martial nature. The Chaldeans, and generations of astrologers who came after them, attributed war to Mars, ostensibly because it was red like blood; but there may also have been deeper reasons, which they doubtless did not have the means to express clearly.

Planetary symbolism is very powerful: it is the core of astrology and has even become part of our own everyday language. One has only to look at definitions in a dictionary:

saturnine: supposed to be under the influence of the planet Saturn, which tends to make people morose; morose, of a gloomy temper; heavy; grave; phlegmatic.
martial: from Mars, the god of war; pertaining to war; suited to war; military; given to war; warlike.
jovial: (because the planet Jupiter was believed to make those born under it of a jovial temperament) gay; merry; joyous; jolly.[9]

This symbolism can be found among the Greeks in the works of Ptolemy, the 'prince of astrologers',[10] in the Arab authors of the middle ages, in Paracelsus at the time of the Renaissance, and in the more humble astrological tracts of the twentieth century. Saturn sombre and melancholy; Jupiter jovial and powerful; Mars quarrelsome; the Moon dreamy; Venus seductive – these definitions seem remarkably similar to my own descriptions of the influence of the planets on personality. It could indeed be that my statistical work, with the vast catalogue of 50,000 personality traits, will rehabilitate this ancient planetary system.

I touched on the matter in 1973, in my book *Cosmic Influences on Human Behaviour*.[11] As an example, I cited an Elizabethan comedy by John Lyly, *The Woman in the Moone*, whose scenario is an excellent summary of planetary symbolism. In the story,

Pandora is led to take on successively the character corresponding to the Sun, the Moon and the seven planets.[12] 'This astrological comedy', I wrote, 'compels us to ask ourselves some
pointed questions of the relationship between our work and
astrology. The gloomy, melancholy mood which engulfed Pandora when Saturn took over her soul; the ambition and pride
which Jupiter bestowed; the quarrelsome aggressiveness which
accompanied the arrival of Mars – all these traits confirm our
observations . . . astrological "mentalities" are "surprising".'[13]
However, I was being a little too optimistic when I promised 'to
return to this question soon in order to establish an objective
parallel between each astrologer's opinion on the attributes of
the planets and the results of our statistics'.[14]

In 1977 I suggested to Françoise Gauquelin that she undertake
the investigation, or rather, persuaded her to do so: she was far
from convinced (and a great deal less than I was) about the
reality of astrological planetary symbolism. After a brief perusal
of astrological treatises, she still believed that the example of
Mars and its 'martial' nature, which we had in fact observed in
persons born at the rise or culmination of the planet, was no
more than a coincidence, just another instance of the discrepancy between astrology and our results. With my greater knowledge of astrology and less hostile attitude, I remained relatively
sanguine about the eventual outcome of the inquiry.

Françoise Gauquelin plunged into my library of astrological
works, a fairly extensive collection ranging from Manilius'
Astronomicon and Ptolemy's *Tetrabiblos*, written in the pre-
Christian era, to the latest fashionable book. Each volume was
examined for any account of the planets it contained, and for the
degree of clarity and synthesis employed by the astrologer,
whatever its original language or length. Finally, Françoise
Gauquelin transcribed the opinions of 70 astrologers concerning
the influence of the Sun, the Moon and the planets on personality.

The product of all this painstaking work was, in effect, an
accumulation of tens of thousands of character traits. It was then
necessary to go through the sayings of each astrologer and test
the validity of the description for each planet against our own

reservoir of birth dates and character traits. To give an example of the mode of operation, a certain astrologer associates the Moon with the following character traits – 'imagination, longing for change, passivity, docility, intuition, altruism, dreamer, timidity, inconstancy, frivolity, indecision, indolence, capriciousness, etc.' Most of the lunar traits can be found in our catalogue of 50,000 cases, where they have been retained. In the case of each one, we had noted the position of the Moon at the births of people in our biographical lists to whom this trait was attributed – all this being done quite objectively years before the present project.[15] Having examined the traits described by astrologers in this way, one is then in a position to establish the distribution of the Moon in its diurnal movement at the birth of all the holders of 'astrologically' lunar traits. If the Moon is more often found in excess after its rise or its passage to the meridian – a position of high intensity – the astrologer's profile confirms our observations; in other words, astrological symbolism and our results agree. If, on the other hand, the Moon is distributed regularly throughout all the sectors of its daily movement, the astrologer has failed. Using this technique, we analysed the description of the Moon type according to each of the 70 astrologers, followed by those of the other planets. It was a large undertaking, and we were helped once again by Neil F. Michelsen, president of Astro Computing Services, San Diego, California. With his data-processing machine, which already had the 50,000 character traits and 16,000 births of well-known figures stored in the memory bank, work proceeded rapidly. We also had the assistance of Thomas Shanks, research director of Astro Computing Services, who designed the information programmes for the inquiry.

The outcome was enough to convince us: astrological symbolism seems to be statistically demonstrated, at least for the planets we had previously observed as having some influence on personality, that is, the Moon, Venus, Mars, Jupiter and Saturn. The majority of character traits which astrologers attribute to these planets can be found in the type-lists, compiled before we had thought of testing the claims of astrology. And it cannot be denied that the character traits described by astrologers occur most often when the 'appropriate' planet is rising, passing the meridian, or setting.

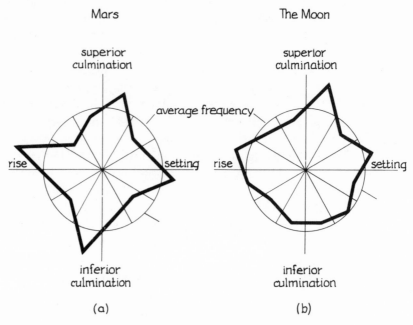

Figure 23 Examples confirming planetary symbolism
Source: F. Gauquelin, *Traditional Symbolism in Astrology,* series D, vol. VII
(1980)

Figure 23 illustrates the exciting conclusions of the investigation with two examples. The astrologer chosen for the purpose is the Englishman, Jeff Mayo, director of an important, and serious, school of astrology and fully representative of the tradition.[16] Figure 23a shows the distribution of the planet Mars in the 12 sectors of its daily movement at the birth of people having, according to their biographies, the character traits astrologers attribute to Mars; figure 23b does the same for the Moon. Taking the circles as indicating average frequency, it is apparent that these two patterns closely resemble those observed empirically at an earlier stage of our work, when astrological tradition was completely ignored (see chapter 4). Those people with 'Mars' or 'Moon' personalities, according to astrologers, had in fact chosen to come into the world in greater numbers when the planet Mars or the Moon was rising or culminating. (The results for Mars are more clear-cut, however.) Statistical analysis showed that chance could not be responsible for so

many points of similarity, and the 'success' of this particular
astrologer where Mars and the Moon were concerned was repeated with many others. In short, the experiment demonstrated in
the clearest possible way that the symbolism of the Moon,
Venus, Mars and Saturn corresponds to a scientifically observable, and even to some extent measurable, reality.

Measurable also means variable. It is noticeable, for instance,
that in the case of the planet Mars the symbolism seems to be
entirely right: the martial nature of the subjects of Paul Couderc's 'rock called Mars' was borne out in every particular. For
the other planets, however, there is greater or lesser correspondence, and it appears to be in relation to Jupiter (and Saturn)
that the divergence with empirical observation is most marked.
On the whole, astrologers have accurately observed the antago-
nism between externalized Jupiter and inward-turned Saturn.
But they trail along with them all sorts of wrong notions, principally centred on Jovian benevolence and Saturnine malevol-
ence, which nothing seems to confirm. Nevertheless, it should
be remembered that our research has by no means exhausted the
subject.

Jupiter, in particular, was disappointing and, on the surface,
hardly favourable to the astrologers. The 'benevolence' and
'wisdom' of Jupiter, which they talk about in astrological tracts,
is only rarely an attribute of people born under that planet. And
yet, some of the character traits mentioned repeatedly by astrologers seemed extraordinarily right. So we had the idea of dividing the traits attributed to Jupiter into two categories,
depending on whether they were associated with a 'well-
aspected' or 'badly-aspected' planet. When Jupiter was favourably situated in the horoscope, according to the astrologers, the
Jovian qualities would be fully evident (piety, benevolence, gen-
erosity, etc.); but when Jupiter was badly placed, the faults
would dominate (pride, extravagance, authoritarianism, etc.).
The results of our experiment were both amusing and instructive. Among the subjects of our inquiry, only the 'bad' Jupiters
were born in any great number under the planet, while the
'good' were not at all.[17] This does not mean, of course, that all
Jupiter types are 'nasty', simply that astrologers have an incomplete view of the symbolism of Jupiter. Sometimes they see
clearly what Jovians are like, at others they cannot see properly

at all. Astrological intuition suffered some reverses with Jupiter
but, even in this case, it could be shown up in the statistics, as
long as the analysis of results was refined.[18]

How accurate are the astrologers when examined in relation to
each other? Françoise Gauquelin has studied this question in
depth.[19] Basically, however, astrological symbolism has
remained constant through the ages, despite a radical change in
language and style between Ptolemy and the modern astrologer.
Certainly, there are astrologers who 'do better' and others who
do less well; but the differences are not always significant and
usually balance out. Some astrologers have improved with time,
others have got worse. Notoriety is no guarantee of a better
result, and originality often takes the author further off target.
Indeed, popular books written for easy money, which lift traditional symbolism intact, receive excellent 'scores' in our observations.

So, the symbolism was confirmed for five of the planets, but
we naturally wondered how it would fare with the remaining
five – Mercury, Uranus, Neptune, Pluto and the Sun itself.[20]
We decided that it would be interesting to compare the astrologers' interpretation with our catalogue of 50,000 character
traits, and proceeded in exactly the same way. From the results
produced by the computer, the frequencies observed were not
significant and were often incoherent.[21] Nonetheless, we intend
to carry the investigation further.

Paradoxically, the worst results were for the Sun itself,
although tradition on the subject is rich and consistent. One may
assume that astrologers, understandably impressed by the Sun,
credited it with influences on personality which it simply does
not have. The failure, or the illusion if you prefer, may well lie
in the fact that the Sun is not a planet but a star. Solar influence
is extremely strong on the Earth and on ourselves, physically
speaking; yet its 'astrological' role is strangely dumb compared
with the planets, even though these represent relatively nil in
terms of energy emitted.

Astrology is a game of mirrors: you look at a mystery, it reflects
another. Its status is unique in the scale of scientific values. A

large part of its planetary symbolism has been demonstrated to be incontrovertibly, statistically true. But, at the same time, the zones of daily movement of the planets to which astrologers attribute the most influence are not necessarily the correct ones. And so you have the astrologer with right ideas about planetary influences, bent over a horoscope which will give a false reading, because for him the planet is 'strong' in the sky where in reality it is 'weak'. Who can tell the origin of this uncertain balance, this rickety astrological truth?

7

The Horoscope Falls Down

Astrological tradition is not limited to the planets, Sun and Moon. There is also the zodiac, whose 12 signs represent the most well-known and widely applied aspect of astrology.

When I started my statistical control of astrological laws in 1950, I turned naturally to the zodiac. But the results have been consistently disappointing, in terms both of the influence of the zodiac on professional success and of zodiacal heredity between parents and children. My observations, published in 1955 and again more recently, attracted some criticism from astrologers.[1] The burden of their complaint was that they could not accept the negative verdict of statistics, unless I could prove case by case – with the help of biographies, for instance – the absence of zodiacal influences.

Zodiacal symbolism is very well defined. As they pass through the 12 signs, the Sun, Moon and planets exert different influences, since each of the signs – Aries, Taurus, Gemini, Cancer, Leo, Virgo, Libra, Scorpio, Sagittarius, Capricorn, Aquarius and Pisces – is itself related to a personality type. For example, a typical description of Aries, first sign of the zodiac, is: 'His principal qualities are courage, will-power, independence, a taste for adventure. His faults are that he is incapable of staying in one place and is impulsive. Aries is ambitious, energetic.'

This is, in fact, a precise psychological profile, built up on a number of character traits. Now, with my catalogue of 50,000 character traits, plus all the corresponding zodiacal positions stored in the memory bank of the computer, I had an excellent opportunity for testing zodiacal symbolism and submitting it to the same kind of strict analysis carried out by Françoise Gauquelin on planetary symbolism.

The procedure for the experiment was to list all the character traits that astrologers attributed to each sign of the zodiac. I then referred to the people in my statistics showing characteristics of a sign – it might be Aries, for example – to see whether they were born more often 'under this sign' than the others (or, to be more technically precise, if the particular sign was more strongly marked on their horoscope). I repeated the process for each sign and according to each astrologer, using the same astrological works as those in the earlier investigation of planetary symbolism. With the help of the computer at Astro Computing Services, I examined the presence of the Sun, and also of the Ascendant, the Moon and the planets in the 12 signs.

This time, the results which came out of the computer were completely unfavourable to astrological tradition.[2] This inquiry into character-traits and the signs of the zodiac led to the same results as those carried out into the professions and heredity and the zodiac: it ended in total failure for the astrology of the signs of the zodiac. People attributed with Aries characteristics, for instance, were born quite as often under the other 11 signs; and the same held true for Taurus, Gemini, and so on right through to Pisces. Sometimes, of course, a more significant result would emerge from the mass of data, but it rarely conformed with the sign and might even contradict it. Chance ruled everywhere.

Figure 24 illustrates the result for the Sun and for the Ascendant in relation to the signs of Aries and Virgo. Once again, I have drawn on the work of Jeff Mayo to represent the astrological tradition (see also figure 23).[3] Where the zodiac is concerned, however, astrologers are extremely coherent, even strict, and there is little variation between them. The general tendency of each sign is fairly constant, although the terms used to express it may differ.

Figures 24a and b refer to Aries, showing separately the distribution of the Sun and of the Ascendant through the 12 signs, at the birth of people having Aries character traits according to their biographies. Given that the circles indicate the average frequency of births, it is clear that 'Aries types' did not choose to come into the world in any great numbers when the Sun or

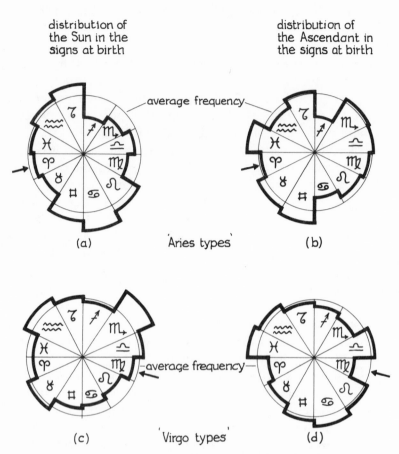

distribution of
the Sun in the
signs at birth

distribution of
the Ascendant in
the signs at birth

average frequency

(a)   'Aries types'   (b)

average frequency

(c)   'Virgo types'   (d)

Figure 24   Examples of the invalidity of zodiacal symbolism
Source: M. Gauquelin, *Zodiac and Character-traits*, series D, vol. VIII (1981)

the Ascendant was in Aries. The figure also shows two maxima
for the Sun, one in Cancer, the other in Capricorn, while the
Ascendant was particularly frequent in Gemini and Pisces.
These variations are not abnormal on the statistical level, and
they also conflict utterly with the psychology of the signs in
question.

Figures 24c and d give the same demonstration for the sign of
Virgo. Again, it can be seen that 'Virgo types' were born slightly
less often than average with the Sun in this sign, while there is a
certain increase in Scorpio; as for the Ascendant, it actually
occurred least often of all in Virgo at the birth of people whose
behaviour was compatible with this sign.

One could extend the investigation to all the signs of the zodiac and use other astrological works, but it is doubtful whether these initial observations would improve, especially as astrological interpretation is so uniform on the subject. Moreover, I had already analysed thousands of character traits for the experiment. The only conclusion is that the influence of the signs of the zodiac is not confirmed by an objective study of the behaviour of thousands of people – or, to put it crudely, the signs of the zodiac are valueless. In the way that astrologers interpret them, and to the extent one can speak of an ideal negative proof, that much is certain. Even the quality of the experimental population is beyond reproach, for it was on that very basis, using the same reservoir of character traits, that planetary symbolism was so strikingly demonstrated.

Perhaps a more searching analysis of the data from the zodiac inquiry would reveal other 'heterodox' influences. With that in mind, I decided to experiment with the 'sidereal' zodiac. This system, dear to some Anglo-Saxon astrologers, takes into account the astronomical phenomenon of the precession of the equinoxes, and is therefore some 20 degrees different along the ecliptic from the traditional zodiac. But the results were no more interesting.[4] A study of the data using a division of the zodiac into 36 (as opposed to 12) sectors, which astrologers call 'decanates', ended in failure too.

Some more skilful researcher may find a method of demonstrating scientifically the signs of the zodiac, but it is more a pious hope than an expectation. And the astrologer's sense of duty should spur him to an agonizing revision of his ideas: a horoscope without the zodiac is surely like a day without the sun.

Many others, besides and before me, have attempted to verify the claims of astrology. But, owing to scientific prejudice, those who have done so have tended to be sympathetic to the idea. This is unfortunate because, whatever their intellectual integrity, these writers are prone to interpret the results with a bias in favour of the horoscope. In addition, as I know from personal experience, their work is unlikely to be recognized by the scientific community, simply on the grounds that they are known to be astrologers or pro-astrology.

In fact, it was astrologers themselves who first thought of testing the laws of astrology. At the beginning of the twentieth century, Paul Choisnard (1867–1930) formulated numerous experiments to show the influence of the stars.[5] He carried out several investigations whose results, favourable to the horoscope, were published.[6] A generation later, the Swiss Karl Ernst Krafft (1900–1945) assembled a formidable body of statistics in the case for astrology, in his *Traité d'Astrobiologie*.[7]

In 1955, I presented a thorough analysis of the statistical work of Choisnard and Krafft, to which I refer the reader for greater detail.[8] I found a number of errors in their observations and was unable, in spite of using a much larger sample of births than theirs, to rediscover the 'laws' of astral influence which they claimed to have demonstrated so reliably.[9] Indeed Krafft and Choisnard, long revered by astrologers, have fallen from their pedestals. As Jacques Sadoul remarks in his fully documented book: 'The "scientific" astrology created by Choisnard at the beginning of the century cannot be given serious consideration today.'[10] And of Krafft's monumental *Traité d'Astrobiologie*, nothing remains. These unfortunate pioneers, men of their time, belong to an outdated generation.

The invention and general availability of computers has led to a surge in the number of astrological researchers. There are hundreds all over the world, juggling about with programmes on their mini-calculators to prove this or that astrological law. There has also been a revolution in the style of astrological writing, a switch to a scientific style of presentation in dry, factual language, with figures, graphs and bibliographies.[11]

Most of these 'new astrologers' are English or American, with France lagging far behind. The English Astrological Association has even undertaken a vast project to collect everything published in astrological literature since the beginning of the twentieth century. And it was an Englishman living in Australia, Geoffrey Dean, with the help of his fellow countryman, the astrologer Arthur Mather, who brought out a study of *Recent Advances in Natal Astrology*.[12] Some 600 closely printed pages, it is a bibliographical goldmine for the curious researcher. Reaction to the book has been wide and varied, the sceptics regarding it as too favourable to astrology, and the 'fans' of the horoscope as over-critical.[13] At least it shows that there are people in the astrological world prepared to reassess their ideas and to make use of their critical sense in a positive way, even if they represent a tiny minority. John Addey, another Englishman, is an example. Using my material on births and character traits, he applied the data to his own particular ideas, namely 'harmonics'. Although one might not accept all his conclusions (which incidentally lead to a non-previsional and fairly heterodox astrology), Addey's sincerity and tenacity deserve respect.[14] Astrologers, too, are capable of publishing negative results. An investigation into suicide was set up by members of the National Council of Geocosmic Research (NCGR), under the direction of the American astrologer, Nona Press.[15] The mode of operation conformed to all the standards demanded by scientific method: dates and hours of birth were obtained from the New York register offices; a control group of 'non-suicides' was set up under the same conditions; the causes of suicide were noted down, as well as the precise moment when they took place; all the astronomical parameters of the horoscopes were calculated by computer; appropriate and somewhat specialized statistical methods were employed to analyse the results. It was a model experiment, but the conclusions were entirely negative: the planets had no influence on the fact, manner, or time of suicide. It was courageous to publish a work so unfavourable to astrology.

Again, there was a mixed reaction to Edmund Van Deusen's book, *Astrogenetics*.[16] This claims to be a statistical study of the position of the Sun in the sky at the birth of several thousand people, from various professions taken out of *Who's Who*. The author was convinced that he had proved the influence of the signs of the zodiac on the nature of professional success. His conclusions were accepted in their totality by most astrologers. But some of them, notably Geoffrey Dean, pinpointed the error in the work: like Krafft some 40 years earlier, Van Deusen had taken a demographic law for an astrological law. For my own part, I made the same deduction.[17]

But the best illustration of a critical sense among astrologers is the attitude they finally adopted to the theories of the Czech doctor, Eugen Jonas (needless to say, there are still a number of people who believe that Jonas is right). Dr Jonas maintained that he had perfected an infallible system of astrological control of births. This astrological 'Ogino law' was essentially based on the cosmic positions, particularly of the Moon, at the moment of conception. Jonas also said he could predict the sex of the child with a 99 per cent chance of success, if he knew the zodiacal sign that the Moon was in at the moment of conception, and that he could define in advance the good health and constitution of the child. A girl or a boy in excellent health and when you want, without any of the inconveniences of the Pill – these were seductive claims; and the fact that Jonas was on the other side of the Iron Curtain, and that the institute for the practical application of his ideas, *Astra,* had been closed by the Czech authorities, added a touch of martyrdom. Astrologers everywhere began to talk about Jonas and to deplore his fate. A book was written about him.[18]

However, some researchers were not content with blind acceptance of Jonas's discoveries and wanted to test their validity. The most important verification was carried out by the Americans R. Kimball and W. H. Kautz and took three years. In a sample of 500 women who had followed the Ogino astrological method, the failure rate was remarkable; in 400 cases, the sex of the child was compared with the position of the Moon at the moment of conception. Correct diagnoses were not 99 per cent but nearer 50 per cent, that is to say on the average.[19] Other astrologers have performed experiments and received no better results. Enthusiasm for Jonas's ideas is now a thing of the past and, within ten years, astrologers have managed to rid their doctrine of a false theory which at one time threatened to take root – which must be to their credit. Are false notions rejected so quickly when they run wild in medicine, physics or astronomy?

If astrology is potentially a science, then it demands extra caution in field research. One must never lose sight of the possibility of 'alternative explanations', as the scientific jargon has it;[20] and this involves finding out whether positive results can be accounted for logically and simply, quite apart from any astrological law.

A few years ago Jeff Mayo, the English astrologer mentioned earlier (see chapter 6), approached the psychologist, Hans Eysenck, with a suggestion. He wanted to compare the answers to a personality questionnaire drawn up by Eysenck with certain factors of the horoscope.[21] Eysenck was interested, and Mayo proceeded to obtain answers to the questionnaire from over 2,000 men and women. Observing the distribution of the Sun in the 12 signs, he noticed a correlation between its position and the extroversion (or introversion) aspect shown on the questionnaire. This discovery complied with an astrological law stating that the even signs are masculine, positive and exteriorized (Aries, Gemini, Leo, Libra, Sagittarius, Aquarius), while the odd signs are feminine, negative and interiorized (Taurus, Cancer, Virgo, Scorpio, Capricorn, Pisces). After calculating the average for extroversion on the questionnaire for all the Aries people, followed by the Taureans and so on through the signs, Jeff Mayo ended up with 12 values. Placing these along a straight line representing the average, he found that there was a regular zig-zag, going up with an extrovert note at each even sign and down at the next odd sign. The phenomenon applied equally to men and women.

Hans Eysenck was informed and he and his statistician, Owen White, agreed to add their names to Mayo's in the published account of the experiment in a psychological journal.[22] Eysenck did not necessarily share all the conclusions of the article; but his signature was intended to encourage others – non-astrologers if possible – to control the experiment using fresh material. It caused a stir because of Eysenck's standing: astrologers were delighted, psychologists were generally disapproving. And work was soon completed which appeared to invalidate Mayo's observations, notably by Jackson and Fiebert in the USA, Veno and Pamment in Australia, and Saklofske, Kelly and McKerracher in Canada.[23]

So Eysenck, whom I knew through a collaboration of several years' standing, asked me to verify Mayo's results on a group of French male and female subjects. I gave Eysenck's questionnaire to over 600 subjects and compared their score on the test with the solar position at their birth, but failed to find any trace of Mayo's famous zig-zag. It was obviously essential to seek an 'alternative explanation' for Mayo's initial results, which had seemed so favourable to astrology but had not proved reproducible.

At this stage, Eysenck returned to an earlier criticism of

Mayo. He had been accused of not using a 'chance' population for his experiment, but one that represented almost the entire student body of his college of astrology. These were 'apprentices' in effect, who knew their own birth signs and had already acquired some knowledge of the interpretation of signs from their astrology classes. Like 'good students', they may well have unconsciously provoked Mayo's results by identifying themselves with their birth signs when answering the questionnaire. With Mayo's help, Eysenck now divided all the respondents to the questionnaire into three groups, depending on their astrological ability – highly competent; knowing only the signs of the zodiac; completely ignorant. At a symposium on 'Astrology and Psychology', held at the institute of psychiatry of the University of London in May 1979, Eysenck described what happened. The zig-zag effect was evident only in relation to answers from individuals belonging to the second group. The reason, according to Eysenck, was that it was artificially produced by the astrology students, identifying with what they knew to be the character of their own signs. Thus, the results were negative for people in the third group, who were too ignorant to be influenced; there was no effect with the first group either, because its members were too knowledgeable about the horoscope and its mysteries to attach much importance to their sun signs alone.

An experiment by two German researchers, K. Pawlik and L. Buse, had demonstrated the same tendency among people who know their own birth signs and their psychological significance in answering personality questionnaires.[24] As Eysenck concludes, our results 'thus clearly agree with Pawlik and Buse. . . . They suggest that the Mayo study gave positive results because of an inadequate way of assessing knowledge of astrology and there is no real relationship between personality and Sun-signs. The same conclusion must apply to many other studies which have reported positive results, but have not controlled for knowledge of astrology.'[25]

In the Prelude to this book, I mentioned two ways of verifying the validity of astrology – clinical control and statistical experimentation. So far, I have concentrated on the second method, because I regard it as more important. However, most astrologers would disagree, placing little confidence in what are, to them, frequently disappointing reports of statistical inquiries. In their view, the horoscope is a whole, a *gestalt*. As the well-known American astrologer, Zipporah Dobyns, has written: 'He (Gauquelin) commits some of the same errors of over-simplification by refuting various factors singly. Thus he considers signs alone, aspects alone, houses alone, etc., and finds no meaning in them. But the one primary rule in astrology is that no factor can be taken out of context without a real danger of losing the meaningful *gestalt*.'[26] The astronomers, R. B. Culver and P. A. Ianna, reply: 'Scientists cannot help but marvel at a "meaningful *gestalt*" which seems to be lost only when the testing of individual factors in a horoscope yields null results, although a great many experimental and observational scientists have undoubtedly long yearned for the existence of such behaviour in their own areas of endeavour!'[27]

Nevertheless, tests have been devised to measure the astrologer's ability to interpret the *whole* horoscope, an expression of the 'meaningful gestalt'. It is a question of whether this skill, which the practitioner genuinely believes himself to possess, actually exists.

The astrologer-psychologist Vernon Clark, a familiar figure in any defence of astrology, conducted an experiment with some American colleagues, where he asked them to match a certain number of horoscopes with a certain number of descriptions of the professions and lives of individuals.[28] Naturally, he alone knew what the right answers were. In one of the tests, the astrologers were required to find the horoscopes corresponding to a snake breeder, a musician, an accountant, a veterinary surgeon and an art teacher; in another, on female births, they had to do the same for a writer, a librarian, an artist, a prostitute and a doctor. 'Such information seems to me hardly sufficient to carry out Vernon Clark's test,' writes Jacques Sadoul. 'It was only a question of guesswork, and one could answer anyhow!'[29] Yet, the American astrologers were remarkably successful in passing the test.

Frankly, I don't think Clark's test proves anything. For instance, he refers to a successful experiment with 50 astrologers from England, the USA and elsewhere without giving their names, thereby making it impossible to measure their skill again in a second test along the same lines. Moreover, the French astrologers who tried Clark's test – all serious professionals – failed it completely. Paul Colombet, president of the Centre International d'Astrologie, explains:

> This test seems to be based on a fundamental fault: it provides us with a purely external picture of each subject, whereas experience has taught us that astrology is above all the reflection of an internal reality, and that one must first of all define that before risking any conjectures about its realization in external life. We were surprised that our friends at *In Search* (the American astrological journal where Vernon Clark's experiment was published) did not put Vernon Clark on his guard against this remarkable lack of psychology in a psychologist. . . . This test is not fundamentally in tune with the normal practice of astrology.[30]

Vernon Clark has since died, and I never had the opportunity of asking him about the reasons for the success of the English-speaking astrologers. However, Jacques Sadoul reports the reaction of the American astrologist, Dal Lee, to the test:

> The test consisted in ten pairs of horoscopes. We were asked to sort them into the right pairs. . . . There was a date by which the answers were to be sent back. I was extremely busy at the time at the magazine, and I put the test to one side, and finally the day came when it had to be sent back. In principle, it should have taken an astrologist at least half an hour to evaluate each theme, that is to say, ten hours in all. I decided to give each horoscope precisely one minute, thus 20 minutes overall, and I sent off my answers to Mr Clark. When the results were published, I found out that I had been right for the first seven dates, and wrong for the last three. My result was thus felt to be above the level of chance and thus valid. But, for myself, I could not consider it as purely astrological because I only gave a minute to each theme. I believe rather that it was a case of 'extra-sensory perception', and that would also explain why, as I grew tireder, my 'extra-sensory perception' did not allow me to find the right date for the last three pairs of horoscopes.

As Jacques Sadoul remarks: 'It is obvious that, if a number of other astrologers behaved like Dal Lee, or else used pendulums, or clairvoyance, or whatever, then Clark's tests are singularly diminished in value.'[31] The failure of the French astrologists, clairvoyance or not, remains inexplicable: there is nothing to show that their qualities as practitioners were in any way inferior to those of Vernon Clark's colleagues.

Astrologers sometimes invent tests of the Vernon Clark type, which is entirely to their credit, and the results are usually highly favourable to astrology. One wants to know why. A recent experiment was that by the astrologer, Joseph E. Vidmar, with 28 astrologers participating.[32] Vidmar applied his tests at the National Astrological Society conference, held at Tucson, Arizona, in March 1978 and, as I was there, I had first-hand experience of them. I realized then why this kind of experiment could succeed. It was not a matter of cheating, simply that the tester, as an astrologer himself, selected horoscopes to match the personality and destiny of their possessors. The investigator was not to blame: he believed himself to be reasoning correctly. But the fact that the astrologers gave the right answers was only a certificate of their expert knowledge of the rules, not a proof that their art is a science. Indeed, as long as tests of this type are left to the initiative of astrologers themselves, there will always be doubts about their authenticity as proof. The ideal solution would be for someone both competent and impartial, but outside the astrological environment, to undertake such a venture.

Over the years, I have tested astrologers (whose anonymity they have asked me to preserve), generally at their own request. The basic model is to present them with 20 horoscopes, 10 belonging to people who have some striking characteristic in common, the other 10 to people with the opposite characteristic. The astrologer has to match the horoscopes with the characteristics in question as correctly as possible. For instance, there might be 10 horoscopes of nonagenarians and 10 horoscopes of children who died in infancy; 10 of criminals and 10 of non-criminals; 10 of mentally ill people and 10 of people recognized as sane; 10 of people who died a violent death and 10 of people who died in their beds; and so on. I have to admit that astrologers regularly fail these tests and are sometimes so disillusioned that they accuse me of rigging the cases.

Astrologers can justifiably argue that their clients are satisfied, otherwise they wouldn't return for more; they see this as further proof of their ability to interpret horoscopes properly. And, to a large extent, people are impressed by the accuracy of psychological portraits which astrologers draw from their 'charts'.

There is a feeling of near reverence for astrological knowledge and, some years ago, I decided to investigate it.[33] I placed an announcement in the press:

ABSOLUTELY FREE!
Your ultra-personal horoscope
A 10-PAGE DOCUMENT
Benefit from a unique experiment
Send name, address, date and
place of birth to: ASTRAL ELECTRONIC.

My advertisement drew a large response. To the first 150 who replied, I sent the same psychological analysis – a true interpretation by an authentic astrologer of the horoscope of a person who had actually existed. It belonged, in fact, to a celebrated French criminal, Dr Petiot, who had murdered over fifty people during the Second World War, although neither the astrologer nor 'my' clients knew his identity.

I received a dozen enthusiastic letters of acknowledgement.[34] Ninety per cent thought that the portrait was very true and expressed their personal difficulties well, while for 80 per cent this favourable judgement was shared by family and friends. Psychologists have taught that we all tend to see a mirror of ourselves in the horoscope;[35] but it is still disquieting that these people should find a resemblance in a profile drawn to fit only one individual – a murderer.

Ray Hyman, professor of psychology at the University of Oregon, has written a classic analysis of 'cold readings'.[36] He exposes techniques for manipulating people into providing a picture of their personality which will strike them with its accuracy, when it is just a generally applicable text skilfully put together. In 1948, Bertram Forer created a psychological portrait from a 'news stand astrology book', which he tested on his students. It reads:

Some of your aspirations tend to be pretty unrealistic. At times, you are extroverted, affable, sociable, while at other times you are introverted, wary and reserved. You have found it unwise to be too frank in revealing yourself to others. You pride yourself on being an independent thinker and do not accept others' opinions without satisfactory proof. You prefer a certain amount of change and variety, and become dissatisfied when hemmed in by restrictions and limitations. At times you have serious doubts as to whether you have made the right decision or done the right thing. Disciplined and controlled on the outside, you tend to be worrisome and insecure on the inside.

As Hyman comments: 'Forer's students, who thought the sketch was uniquely intended for them as a result of a personality test, gave the sketch an average rating of 4·26 on a scale of 0 (poor) to 5 (perfect). . . . Almost 30 years later, students give the same sketch an almost identical rating as a unique description of themselves. . . . In the case of cold reading, the manipulator may be conscious of his deception; but often he too is a victim of personal validation.'[37]

Hyman's demonstration does not apply to astrology alone, but it is convincing. The satisfaction which people feel in reading their horoscopes does not prove the validity of astrology. 'Know yourself,' said Socrates, 'and you will know the secret of the gods.' But who can boast of having managed it? Certainly not the clients of astrologers.

I conclude this study of the confrontation between the laws of astrology and my observations with the words of a sceptical writer, Anthony Standen. He seems to have summed up the paradoxical situation in which I find myself:

But (assuming that his claims are true) has Gauquelin really 'proved' astrology? It depends on what you mean – 'astrology'. If you mean ordinary conventional astrology, which is current in this country (the USA) and in many others, and is so prevalent nowadays that no one can possibly escape it, then Gauquelin has utterly and completely disproved it. But if you are going to call by the name 'astrology' *any* effect that is found that depends on the planets and is unexplained by science, never mind whether it

agrees with conventional astrology or is entirely different, then
Gauquelin makes a very strong claim to have found such a
thing.[38]

Standen adds: 'There are a number of reasons why Gauquelin's claims are received with utter and complete scepticism.
What sort of influences do we get from the planets anyway?' It
is a good and difficult question, which I will try to answer in the
next chapter.

8

'Midwife' Planets?

To give an explanation, whether scientific or not, of all the influences contained in a horoscope is an impossible task. Thankfully, it is not my problem, since the 'neo-astrological' effects I have discovered are a good deal more limited in number than those of the horoscope, and their nature is rather different. Nevertheless I am confronted with the vast difficulty of trying to propose a coherent scientific model capable of accounting for my observations.

'What?' objects the scientist, 'you claim that if a child is born when Mars is rising, then he will be gifted with greater energy than other men, and his chances of succeeding in sport will be the more increased?' Apparently, my planetary effects belong to the same category of 'absurdity' that embraces astrology as a whole. Indeed, the child comes into the world fully formed, with all its potential gifts inherited from its parents; and it is hard to accept that a planet, acting on the chromosome structure of the cells, should shake them up and redistribute them in such a way as to give a decisive orientation to its character.

But, if a physical explanation of the phenomenon is absolutely necessary, it seems to me that the only approach is to link it with the role of heredity. That is why I attach so much importance to the series of results which I have called 'the planetary effect on heredity' (discussed in chapter 2). Its fundamental characteristic is that, if the father (or mother) is born with the Moon or a planet (Venus, Mars, Jupiter or Saturn) in the key sectors of rise or culmination, the child tends to come into the world with the same planet in the same key sectors of the sky, more often than is the case with other children.

Around 1960, when my early observations seemed to point to this relationship between planets and heredity, I began to haunt the medical faculty library of the University of Paris, systematically reading everything which might provide the answer to two questions – how does childbirth start? and, does the foetus play a role during childbirth? I already knew that it was through the intermedium of heredity in the child that the planetary effect manifested itself, and I had a fairly clear idea of the problem, as expressed in my book of 1966:

> Carrying a burden of heredity, both paternal and maternal, the child seems to be sensitive, at the moment of birth, to the subtle solicitations of cosmic space. It reacts selectively, in function of the elements of its constitution, inherited sometimes from its father, and sometimes from its mother. . . . Let us hope that the development of the science of childbirth will ratify this view in the future. It is up to the specialists to clarify the question of the possible role played by the infant during the physiological processes which bring about the moment of its arrival in the world.[1]

But, in all the literature I studied at this time, the conclusion was unanimous and thoroughly discouraging for me: the foetus could play no role in its entry into the world. Authors derided Hippocrates' assertion of some 2,500 years ago: 'When the time is ripe, the child moves, breaks the membranes holding it in and leaves its mother's womb.' For, as Aidan Macfarlane has written: 'The body of scientific opinion during the last century and the earlier part of this one promoted the idea of the uterus as a fortress, impregnable to anything other than sperm. The uterus was pictured as a kind of mausoleum entombing the foetus within it. There was no internal or external stimulation of any kind until, at the end of the nine months, life suddenly burst out.'[2]

Then, suddenly, a veritable revolution took place, owing to the progress of medical research and, within 20 years, the reverse theory has gained widespread acceptance among specialists. Professor Robert Debré, of the Académie de Médecine, sums it up: 'It is the foetus which tells the mother when to expel it!'[3] After all, it seems as though Hippocrates wasn't quite as stupid as some may have thought – nor, indeed, was my own idea.

Opening a symposium on 'Foetal Autonomy' in December 1968, the chairman, Dr G. S. Dawes, claimed: 'Finally, there is evidence that suggests that the foetus normally initiates the process of parturition, thus liberating itself from the intra-uterine environment which has protected it.'[4] The mechanisms now considered to explain the role of the foetus are related to hormonal changes. The *Medical News Tribune* reported on the work of Dr Liggins, professor of gynaecology and obstetrics at Auckland University, New Zealand: 'Dr G. C. Liggins believes that babies "signal" when they want to be born by releasing prostaglandins which trigger the labour process.'[5] Liggins's research work was concerned with sheep, but he states: 'We know that this applies to human babies as well as animals.' Describing his discoveries, Liggins writes: 'What we show first is that if you destroy the foetal pituitary and remove its adrenal glands which direct the hypothalamus, labour in the sheep does not occur and the pregnancy will continue for months after term.' He maintains that 'the various foetal organs transmit information to the hypothalamus when they have developed to a point which permits survival in the outside world. This begins a process which eventually results in prostaglandin release into the uterine tissue, which triggers contraction and the onset of labour.' In conclusion, Dr Liggins affirms that, as his work has demonstrated, the 'foetal baby does play a big part in the onset of labour.'[6]

Other research has confirmed Liggins's findings, and Macfarlane accurately summarizes the current medical view: 'It is now thought that, when the brain of the baby reaches a certain state of maturity, it releases a substance that begins a chain reaction finally leading to delivery.'[7] Dr Fritz Fuchs, head of the department of obstetrics and gynaecology at the medical college of Cornell University, New York, goes further: 'We don't get unduly alarmed if an unborn child waits for two or three weeks past the calculated due date to trigger his birth. I'm afraid there are a lot of doctors who don't realize the significance of these findings. These doctors continue to suppress or induce labour, sometimes to the baby's detriment. The unborn child is often the best monitor of his own situation. And in the end it is his brain that actually controls his own birth.'[8]

Medical research has also shown that the foetus possesses the capacity, hitherto unsuspected, of reacting to certain outside influences. Life before birth is certainly richer than was thought earlier and, thanks to technical developments, it is possible to observe the activities of the foetus in its mother's womb. The foetus moves, that much was known. But, in addition, from the eleventh week it is able to swallow and then to have hiccups or urinate. It can respond if touched. Its eyes move and one can see on its face various different expressions, such as a smile and even a laugh. It is believed that it dreams. It hears external sounds, of course, but 'tests also showed that babies responded to low frequencies – so low that they could not be appreciated by the human ear and so must have been acting at some other point on the babies' bodies.'[9] In short, 'The baby in the uterus lives in a warm, noisy and maybe pink-tinted world cushioned by surrounding fluid . . . Many influences are at work within this small world. The external environment – be it the far-distant planets or the more immediate social, cultural and physical environment of the mother – plays a part, directly or through the mother.'[10]

Armed with these discoveries, I pursued my explanatory model of planetary influences – or the theory of 'midwife planets', as I called it. The foetus at term would be endowed with a 'planetary sensibility', which would stimulate its entry into the world at a given moment in the daily course of this or that planet, rather than at some other time. This planetary sensibility would be of genetic origin, and the planet itself would not modify the organism of the newborn child. Instead, it would act as the 'trigger', the 'activator' in parturition, while its position in the sky would simply reflect the psychobiological temperament of the child.

It is well known in medicine that it takes only the tiniest thing to trigger off labour. A specialist, J. D. Ratcliffe, has written: 'One part adrenalin in 400 million parts of blood is enough to cause a specific reaction in a human being.'[11] This 'tiny thing' could be linked, in part, to subtle cosmic factors surrounding the birth. The child would react to a cosmic 'indicator', led by its hereditary type to be more susceptible to that than to any other.

But what happens when the role of the foetus is rendered inactive, that is when the doctor modifies the normal process of labour, either by surgical intervention (Caesarian) or by introducing a chemical into the maternal organism? In this case (already mentioned in chapter 2), the hereditary effect of the planet disappears: medical interference annihilates the influence of the cosmic indicator. Where childbirth 'by appointment' is concerned, the position of the planet at birth can apparently no longer give any indication of the personality of the subject. The awesome implications of modern obstetric policy for 'neo-astrology' will be examined in chapter 9. Meanwhile, the absence of the planetary effect in non-natural births may be taken as a contrary proof of the possible validity of my explanatory model. And this concept of the planet playing the role of activator in birth, as a function of the hereditary sensitivity of the foetus, could serve as a point of departure for the true explanation of planetary effects.

Such a possibility might seem excessively optimistic, and it's a long way from this vague model to a complete scientific explanation of the wealth of astrophysical and biological phenomena, whose existence the model implicitly admits. What is the exact nature of the energy involved? How does the planetary sensitivity of the foetus operate during labour? What kind of incredible power does the foetus at term possess? How can it select from all the thousands of surrounding influences, near and far, the weakest of these energies from a distant planet, as the only one to accord with its temperament?

Darwin was in the habit of noting both the pros and the cons of his theories – a sensible practice and a wise precaution against potential critics. Following his example, I shall discuss the deficiencies of my model and even the improbability of some aspects. The first objection is not only biological but reasonable. If the planets are nothing but triggers of birth, it would seem that the most important time for determining their influence would be at the beginning of parturition – that is, at the onset of labour when the mother felt the first pangs, rather than at the actual moment of birth. After all, the occasion of the birth is no more than the outcome of a series of factors, in addition to the supposed influence of the planets, occurring throughout the labour process – the weight of the child, the age and physical build of its mother, the number of children she has had already, and so on, not to mention the role of the midwife or doctor.

I concentrated my efforts on this problem of locating and identifying the planetary effect at the onset of labour, instead of at the moment of birth. The first hurdle was obtaining the information, which was not, of course, available from birth certificates. Together with my collaborators, I spent many hours consulting the maternity records of the Baudelocque and Créteil hospitals in Paris, ending up with details of the onset of labour for over 20,000 cases.[12]

The results recorded are fairly perplexing. They are positive but, it must be admitted, extremely weak – so weak that it is impossible to know, in the present state of our observations, whether the planetary effect of the triggering of parturition exists. The fact that the beginning of labour is not recorded with the same precision as the moment of birth does not make matters easier. Labour very often starts at night, and the mother has only an approximate idea, usually accurate to within two hours, of the time when she felt the first pangs.[13] Moreover, certain births do not commence in a clearly defined way, but develop out of a series of signals growing stronger.

All in all, this is a difficult field in which to experiment: the means at our disposal are limited; the effects to be ascertained are inconclusive; and the research for data itself poses considerable problems.[14] Nevertheless, it would be of great benefit to my explanatory model if planetary influence could be observed at the beginning of labour as well, and it should certainly be possible. Time will tell.

This was only the first of the obstacles in the way of my frail theory. So far, I have touched on one aspect of the mystery of cosmic power, concerning biological questions and the role of the foetus. But the other side of the coin presents even more of a challenge – the reasoning of astronomy. How can I seriously speak of 'midwife' planets? These bodies are too far away, too small, their influence on man is negligible. The major forces of nature – gravitation, the effects of the tides, electromagnetic waves, and so on – everything argues against the existence of planetary influence at birth.

To take gravitation first, its laws, discovered by Newton, are universal. Each mass in the universe attracts another mass, in function of the inverse square of the distance separating them, multiplied by a quantity G which is the constant of gravitation. For the planetary effect at birth, therefore, gravitation depends on three factors – the mass of the planet, the mass of the child at birth and the distance between the two. What kind of gravitational force could be exerted by the planets on the newborn child?

Lee Ratzan, a mathematician at the New Jersey Medical School, took an original approach to the problem in 1975.[15] According to him, 'The question was posed as to whether or not celestial bodies exert a greater astrological effect on a newborn child (through gravitational attraction) than the attending obstetrician. An extension of this problem is the extent to which tidal forces induced by planetary masses produce differential forces and perturbations on the bloodstream flow and manifest some effect on the psyche of the offspring.' In his demonstration, Ratzan used the following values – an average weight of 3·4 kg for the child, a weight of 100 kg for the obstetrician, and a distance between the child and the obstetrican of either 0·5 metres or 1 metre; for the masses of the planets, he employed the values given by George Abell.[16] After making the calculations, Ratzan concludes:

The Moon exerts the greatest (tidal) force, then Jupiter, then the medical doctor (at 0·5 m), Saturn, Venus, the medical doctor (at 1 m), and Mars. . . . This supports Carl Sagan's contention that Mars produces a smaller attraction on the newborn child than the physician, but the contention is not necessarily true for all the planets. So perhaps the astrologer has a point after all! Planetary forces do exert a (measurable) force on us mortals. But let us keep the forces in perspective. One can calculate the acceleration caused by this force and its displacement on a 3·4 kg object for one second. This displacement caused by gravitational attraction of the moon is of the order of 17 μm = 0·000017 m, or approximately the distance of two red blood cells placed end to end. The tidal forces are of sufficiently small magnitude that they do not disturb the hydrostatic equilibrium, nor are they sufficient to overcome the viscosity of the blood flow.[17]

The astronomers, R. B. Culver and P. A. Ianna, adopted a similar view as a result of their work: 'The tidal forces exerted by the people and objects in the immediate vicinity of the child overwhelm those exerted by all celestial objects, even those old and storied raisers, the Sun and the Moon.'[18] Culver and Ianna extended their calculations this time taking the planet Mars as the basis. In the midst of the controversy over the Mars effect, it could hardly have been a chance selection, although they maintain 'The choice of Mars here as the standard is strictly arbitrary. Because the planet is deemed astrologically significant, it does provide us, however, with a useful point of reference.'[19] The results leave one wondering: given that the force of gravitation exerted by the planet Mars on the child is 1, then that of the Moon is 4,600 times greater, that of Jupiter 46 times greater, that of Venus 27 times greater, and that of Saturn more than three times greater. Under these conditions, why should the famous Mars effect at birth not be 46 times less than the effect of Jupiter, for instance? And why has one never observed the slightest 'neo-astrological' effect for the Sun, whose gravitational influence is 854,000 times greater than that of Mars?

Alternatively, it might be feasible to explain planetary effects in terms of electromagnetic waves. These cover a vast spectrum, extending from gamma rays, via light waves, to radio waves. Could not one find a wavelength whose level of energy would, more than others, account for the effects of the planets on birth? Or else, could one not imagine a type of wave as yet undiscovered, whose properties would justify planetary influence?

In the view of Culver and Ianna none of this is possible: 'The beauty of the concept of the electromagnetic energy spectrum is, of course, that all of its forms of radiant energy can be described by exactly the same mathematical model that is used to describe visible light.' However, 'At the present there is no evidence to support the idea that undiscovered varieties of electromagnetic energy lying outside of the currently known wavelength limits will have fundamentally different properties than their brethren which lie within.'[20] Taking as their standard the electromagnetic energy deriving from the planet Mars, equal to 1, the two astronomers reckon that the energy emitted by the Moon and Venus is noticeably greater, while that coming from Saturn is at least ten times smaller. They also point out that the Sun or the electric light in the labour room both exert on the child an electromagnetic influence hundreds of times greater than that of Mars.

In other words, even if one discovered a new form of energy, it could not explain my results: there is no measurement in common between the intensity of the electromagnetic energy from the planets and their 'neo-astrological' effects at birth.

If we were all blind, we would not be able to see the planets; but our retinas perceive them. Their light is perhaps the only influence on us which astrophysicists are willing to concede. As the spectrum of light given out by each planet does not dominate the same length of light waves, Mars appears slightly red to us, Jupiter bright and Saturn slightly yellow. These differences of colour, according to astronomers, derive from the properties of the soil or the composition of the atmosphere of the planets. Mars is rich in ferrous oxide, hence the slightly rusty aspect which its light reflects from the Sun; Jupiter's atmosphere is brilliant, whereas Saturn's is not, at least not to the naked eye.

Strangely enough, it is the physical appearance of each planet – a 'trick of the light' for astronomers – which still coincides with the sort of influence it is supposed to exert: Mars is red and warlike, Jupiter brilliant, Saturn bilious. In fact, astronomers assert that there is no correlation between the physical properties of the planets and the types of influence I have observed. Thus the Moon, Mercury and Mars can be classified together, all fairly small masses of solid structure, without atmosphere, or nearly so, and their surfaces covered in rocks. Yet, from a 'neo-astrological' point of view, the Moon does not always have the same effects as Mars, and Mercury does not seem to have any at all. To take another example, Jupiter and Saturn are physically alike: they follow each other in the order of planets in the sky, they are the two biggest objects in the solar system, their structure is gaseous and they have strong magnetic fields. But there could not be two more contrasted types of personality than the extrovert Jovians and the introverted Saturnines.

A famous law holds that influences decrease in function of the inverse square of their distance. But even this is not true of the planets. The distance from the planets to the Earth is not constant, owing to astronomical movements, and the variations can sometimes be very marked, as well as perceptible to the naked eye. Venus and Mars, for instance, may be up to several times further away at one time than another, while Venus and Mars appear much larger and brighter when they are closer to the Earth. So, in the course of my study of planetary heredity, I investigated the intensity of the 'Venus effect' and 'Mars effect' at birth, to see whether these varied in function of the distance of the planets from the Earth. I found, unfortunately, that the intensity of the effect is constant for both planets, no matter what their distance – one more anomaly to add to the explanatory model of astral influence.[21]

The planets have other characteristics which fit awkwardly with the current state of our knowledge. The astronomer, Paul Couderc, writes: 'I do not like these planets which act when they are in one part of the sky and do not act at all when they are elsewhere.'[22] He was alluding to the zones of higher intensity which the planet passes through in its daily passage after the horizon and meridian. And it is indeed disconcerting that, during its movement over 24 hours, a planet may be considered 'strong' for some two and a half hours after its rise, then fairly suddenly as less 'strong' until the time when it reaches the superior culmination, where its influence again increases, after which it decreases once more until it sets, and then increases, and so on.

This phenomenon is fundamental, since it describes empirically the laws of planetary intensity during the diurnal movement. It has always irritated biologists and astronomers, who would have found it much easier to accept a theory of progressive intensity, starting at the rise of the planet and reaching its maximum at the superior culmination (like the intensity of the Sun's rays in the course of the day). The true laws, which I have of course observed, are scorned by astronomers as 'the astrological no-man's land'. In the words of Paul Couderc:

I can imagine the anguish of those populations living north of the Polar circle. Let us take the case of Murmansk, a city some 70° north. It is easy to calculate thus: when Mars rises on its trajectory near the winter solstice, this planet must remain for nearly three months without rising over the horizon in Murmansk. In the same way, Jupiter will stay almost 22 months, and Saturn nearly four and a half years without rising. What will happen to the foetus which needs these triggers to be born? Are there great dramas in Murmansk? And do the statistics show any deficiencies at these dates?[23]

It would certainly be interesting to carry out experiments at Murmansk in the extreme (and extremely rare) astronomical and geographical conditions of birth described by Couderc.

Returning to the point of view of the biologists, I have often been questioned about the purpose of the planetary effect at birth and its role in the mechanisms of evolution. 'Nature does not play dice,' said Einstein, meaning that nothing happens in nature without reason; yet the planetary effect at birth seems to be a monstrous caprice. 'Has it been this way since prehistoric times? Did it affect Cro-Magnon man? Neanderthal man? All hominids? Australopithecus? . . . Does it affect all mammals as they are being born?' asks Anthony Standen. For him, my explanatory model is no more valid than the doctrine of natal influence dear to astrologers: 'Both on the when-the-foetus-is-ready theory and on the baby's-first-breath theory, it is equally inexplicable.'[24]

There is, at the very least, one fact which could testify to the physical reality of the planetary effect – the discovery of a probable link between it and the Earth's magnetism. The complicated history of events leading to this revelation begins with the Sun.

It is a strange paradox that the effects of mass and radiation from the Sun easily dominate all the other cosmic influences exerted on the Earth, and that the planets are infinitely weaker in comparison, and yet that, nevertheless, I have been unable to demonstrate a single instance of the Sun affecting births in the same way as the planets. I have certainly tried to identify solar influences when studying professional groups, biographies and parent/child relationships, but to no avail: natal distribution of the Sun remains magnificently in tune with the laws of chance.

The absence of a solar effect was worrying and, as early as the 1960s, I became preoccupied with the problem of showing, somehow, that the Sun did play a part in planetary influence. I was attracted to two phenomena, familiar to scientists but apparently far removed from neo-astrology (doubtless because the ancients were not in a position to measure them) – solar activity and the Earth's magnetic field.

We enjoy its heat in profusion and flourish in its light, but the Sun gives a false impression of constancy. In fact, it is a changeable star, and its brilliance is far from regular. Astrophysicists and radio-astronomers have observed with their telescopes that our star is the seat of intense and permanent activity. In the first place, it is covered with spots, or more exactly, less bright areas which develop on its agitated surface. These do not occur haphazardly throughout the years, and the number of sunspots is subject to periodicity. The Sun is also subject to sudden eruptions called solar flares, during which it hurls more matter and light into space than usual. This turbulent activity rebounds on the Earth and, in particular, influences the magnetic field of our globe.

The Earth's magnetic field is weak (0·3 to 0·4 gauss) – a simple magnet sold as a toy can reach equivalent strength – but it is important. Scientists now realize that terrestrial magnetism is not constant but fluctuating all the time, the principal variations being essentially due to the Sun. Thus, a measurement of the disturbance in the Earth's magnetic field provides an accurate estimate of solar activity during the preceding hours.

Despite their feebleness, these variations can also be felt by living beings, which are highly sensitive machines where their environment is concerned. Life developed in the melting-pot of the Earth's magnetic field and has been lapped in it since the dawn of biological time: it would not be surprising if it has learned to get information from that source. The work of F. A. Brown and of A. S. Presman has shown that humans and animals are capable of reacting to very weak changes in terrestrial magnetism – sometimes less than 0·4 gauss, the average value of the Earth's field.[25] According to Brown, emeritus professor of biology at Northwestern University, they possess a 'biological compass' aimed at orienting them in space, in addition to a 'biological clock' ordering the rhythm of their activities in time. Space and time become two factors of a single unified field. Subconsciously, man is able to sense slight fluctuations in terrestrial magnetism, and perhaps the foetus can too; indeed, when it is on the point of leaving the womb, it is extremely sensitive to variations in its environment.[26]

At the beginning of the 1960s, the theory of planetary heredity began to take shape, and I decided to try a new experiment. I reasoned that some correlation between the planetary effect at birth and the Earth's magnetic disturbance, if it were possible to observe such a thing, would be enough to prove that the planetary effect depended, at least partially, on the Sun. For a start, it would be reassuring to know that planetary influence was under solar control; but, most important, it would confirm the physical nature of planetary effects. So far, planetary influence had been confined to the realm of astrology, where it seemed absurd. But if terrestrial magnetism had any sort of action, however weak, on the intensity of planetary effects, it would demonstrate that these were material and subject to changes in a known physical field. To verify such a link would be a major step forward in understanding planetary correlation. Moreover, the disturbance of the Earth's magnetism is an indisputable physical fact, measured for over a century, at soil level and beneath.

So, it was not difficult to envisage an experiment to test the influence of the geomagnetism in a delivery room. A compass will indicate magnetic north just as well near the bed of a woman in labour as anywhere else, so long as no object interferes with the magnetic needle. And a positive result, in the form of a measurable alteration in the geomagnetism on the planetary effect, would be very significant.

Since 1884, geophysicists have measured daily variations in the earth's magnetism, using a scale known as the International Magnetic Character, abbreviated to Ci.[27] It is graduated from 0·0 to 2·0, 0·0 for the quietest days when the Earth's magnetism is undisturbed because the Sun itself was quiet in the preceding hours, and 2·0 for the days of 'magnetic storms' when spots and flares increased on the Sun during the preceding hours.

In 1964, I noted the value of terrestrial magnetic disturbance at the births of the 16,000 children comprising my initial inquiry into planetary heredity, and then studied the results to see if geomagnetic disturbance had had any influence. I had no idea what I would find – perhaps nothing at all, perhaps a diminution in the effect on days of intense magnetic disturbance, which could have been interpreted as magnetism creating sufficient 'background noise' to disturb the role of the planets or the sensitivity of the foetus at the moment of birth.

In fact, I observed the opposite: the planetary effect is stronger when the geomagnetic disturbance increases. For reasons of objectivity, I had divided the material into two groups – children born on a disturbed day (Ci from 1·0 to 2·0); and children born on a quiet day (Ci from 0·0 to 0·9). The number of hereditary similarities between child and parent was two times greater when the child was born on a day of disturbed magnetism than when it was born on a quiet day (see figure 25). Precise statistics will make the importance of the phenomenon much clearer and are related to planetary observations in key sectors following the rise or superior culmination. Taking 100 to indicate the absence of planetary effect on heredity (in the case of people without parental links), the planetary effect goes down to 105 in children born on quiet days and rises to 110 in children born on a disturbed day. Owing to the quantity of observations, the difference on a statistical level is remarkable.[28]

The result both pleased and disappointed me. All those mysterious planetary effects were no more than the property, previously overlooked, of a well-known physical energy – the electromagnetic field. There would be nothing revolutionary there, no new 'unknown' rays, no 'obscure' field. But, needless to say, if the relation between planetary effect and geomagnetism really did exist, physicists and biologists would have difficulty in giving a detailed explanation of how it worked.

Before I began the experiment, I did not know how the results would turn out. It is important, when working with statistics, to have a precise hypothesis before starting, but that had not been the case. And, altogether, a diminution in the planetary effect on days of magnetic disturbance would have seemed more 'logical' to me than the precise opposite which actually emerged. In 1977, therefore, I welcomed the opportunity to control my observations using the material from the second experiment on heredity, based again on the births of over 16,000 children.

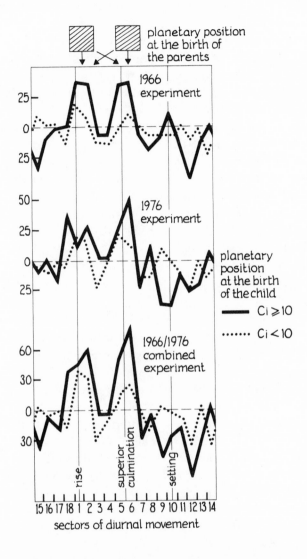

Figure 25 Increase in the planetary effect on heredity with high geo-magnetic activity: combined results for the five major planets
Source: M. and F. Gauquelin, *Replication of the Planetary Effect in Heredity,* series D, vol. II (1977)

Once more, results were stronger for children born on a disturbed day than for those born on a quiet day, although the difference between the two groups of children was less marked this time (see figure 25). It was interesting in both experiments that, while the planet-geomagnetism relation was apparent for Mars, Jupiter and Saturn, it came through most clearly for Venus, but scarcely existed for the Moon.[29]

I attach particular importance to the probable link between the planets and geomagnetism at birth, for the reasons already given. I have several experiments on the subject in progress at my laboratory, as I want to be absolutely sure that the relation exists. The role of geomagnetism remains what is called a second order effect and needs, by definition, a considerable amount of data to prove it. Never has the old adage, 'Science is a long patience', seemed so true.

It can now be said that the planetary sensitivity of the child at birth appears to show itself more easily in a disturbed geomagnetic environment. The discovery of this 'facilitation' marks an important step in understanding the nature, if not the mechanism, of the planetary effect. It also somewhat alters my explanatory model. A more likely hypothesis is that the Sun acts as the motor and the solar field as the medium. The Moon and the closest and most massive planets would cause a disturbance in this field, and the stronger it was, the more intensely it would be felt by the child at its birth. This allows for the fact that the very distant planets like Uranus, Neptune, Pluto and Mercury (the smallest in the solar system) do not reveal any observable influence, perhaps because they are too far away or too small for their disturbance of the solar field to be felt in any significant way by the foetus. In short, the foetus would only be sensitive to the same planets as the retina.

Even if it becomes solidly established, the planet-geomagnetism link at birth is not the ultimate solution and, in one sense, it simply adds another question to all the other unanswered ones. Paul Couderc expresses the almost unanimous opinion of the scientific community:

The new statistical interpretations (put out by Gauquelin) seem to me less unacceptable than the old ones. The planet is no longer to be responsible for the qualities of the newborn child: it has nothing but a triggering role in the births of those sensitive to its presence in certain parts of the sky. Does that mean that I am going to rally to the cause of the role of press-button as the attribute of five planets (including the Moon)? No, I still think that that is giving them too much power, even if one accords them the relay of the solar field. I do not know whether I will live long enough to witness the discovery of an interpretation which will seem likely to me.[30]

I don't know whether I will live long enough myself to see the mystery of astral influence dispelled. The explanation is doubt-less much simpler and much stranger than we can imagine, and perhaps I am making a mistake in trying to rid the planetary effect of all 'absurdity'. The desire to substitute a rational and convincing argument for the astrologers' explanations is laud-able; but I have not forgotten that the road to hell, even the scientific road, is paved with good intentions.

In the end, the facts are always right: the planets have an effect on us, otherwise we would not see them. If the world were populated by blind people, they would deny the existence of light. Our eyes perceive the planets as blue, yellow, and red. So maybe, in its own way and by some quite other channel than the retina, the foetus can tell that it must leave the maternal womb when this 'blue', or 'yellow' or 'red' planet rises or culminates on the horizon, according to its genetic temperament. This is not science fiction or poetic fantasy: nothing is more moving than a birth, nothing more real; and nothing is more majestic than a rising planet, nothing more real. They are two daily, familiar events, where poetry and reality go hand in hand. The only 'scandal' in the eyes of the scientists is the idea of con-nivance between them. Personally, I would welcome a little more curiosity from scientists and a little more reverence for nature, which, has held plenty of surprises since the famous Big Bang. Planetary effects at birth might be one more surprise; the drama comes from our ignorance, after all. When we have greater knowledge, we will be able to judge the concept of 'mid-wife planets', and either dismiss it as crazy or formulate some better explanation.[31]

9

'Neo-Astrology' under Attack

'It seems extraordinary that astrologers base a horoscope which makes predictions for a whole lifetime on the exact time and date of delivery – a time and date that today are more frequently chosen by the obstetrician than by fate.'[1] Thus Aidan Macfarlane pinpoints the principal enemy of research into astral influence – the mechanization of birth – for, as I mentioned in chapter 2, the planetary effect of heredity disappears when delivery is not natural.

Up to about the end of the Second World War, doctors and midwives usually tried not to interfere with birth, preferring to let nature take its course as long as all was going well. The foetus could then play its role of trigger and monitor of the delivery. In the great majority of cases, the position of the planets at the hour of birth corresponded to the genetic temperament of the child and, as soon as it came into the world, a prognosis as to its personality was in theory almost always possible. In the last thirty years, however, medicine has hastened to destroy this link between the child and the planets, discovered after so much difficulty. Indeed, modern obstetrics have become the most formidable opponent of 'neo-astrology', now that the battle against the scepticism of scientists is gradually turning in our favour.

The progressive destruction of neo-astrological data is received with complete indifference by those who should be most alarmed, namely astrologers. They place great importance on knowing the hour of birth, which enables them to build up a comprehensive horoscope, and would really like to have the minute of birth, even the second. But, oddly enough, they show very little interest in the delivery itself, even though this underlies the timing of the birth. What the foetus does in the hours preceding birth in order to bring it to term is of no concern to astrologers, and they regard it as an object without cosmic sensitivity. It is only outside the mother's womb that it is transformed into a person on whom the stars will have conferred a soul, a character and a destiny before he or she has uttered the first cry.

At a recent congress, I raised the whole matter with Zipporah Dobyns, an eminent American astrologer whom I know well. In substance, her reply was: 'Agreed, the planetary effect on heredity disappears in children if the delivery is not natural. But that doesn't matter much because the significance of the horoscope remains valid in any case, whatever the reason for a child's being born at one time rather than another.' In other words, it makes no difference whether nature or the doctor starts off the child's horoscope.

One must understand the reasoning of most astrologers. A horoscope is always in perfect harmony with its owner and in contemporary astrological literature, you will never read of a horoscope being contradicted by the personality or the destiny of the person it was intended for. The doctrine of the 'significant' horoscope reigns supreme: it is one of the principal axioms of astrology, because birth is essentially a question of astral predestination. Whatever the reasons, the year, moment and place of its coming into the world, there exists a sound relationship between the newborn child and the heavens. If the doctor induced the birth of the child on a Friday afternoon say, so that he could get away for the weekend, it scarcely matters to most astrologers. Everything is foreseen, including the doctor's decision or, at least, everything can be accommodated by nature. The Swiss astrologer, Karl Krafft, stated his opinion on this question very clearly, as did Kepler before him.[2] More recently, Carl Gustav Jung has proposed a model for this idea, the theory of synchronicity.[3]

Yet, genetics and foetal medicine have shown that the foetus, carrying its heredity, is already almost a person before birth, with fairly complex physiological and even psychological reactions. This contradicts the astrologers' belief in a total break between 'before' and 'after' birth, with the heavens acting on the child only in the first moment of life. I do not accept that sort of horoscope and I cannot share the indifference displayed by so many astrologers to the 'progress' of obstetrical medicine. If the foetus should leave its mother's womb in its own time, it is surely serious interference to make it be born at another moment.

In the Bible it is written: 'In sorrow shalt thou bring forth children.' Over the centuries, mothers seem to have been victims of this curse, doing little to help the delivery except giving useless cries. But, of course, some deliveries did not go well or continued too long, and mother and child suffered. It was legitimate for doctors to try to correct this, and the idea developed of having the mother participate in the delivery. Psychoprophylaxis was discovered, with the aim of making both pregnancy and delivery an adventure to be actively experienced by the mother.

The method emerged almost simultaneously in the USA and USSR. In the USA, Grantly Dick-Read published *Childbirth Without Fear* in 1933 while, in the 1940s, Fernand Lamaze, a French obstetrician, brought back from the Soviet Union the concept of 'natural childbirth'.[4] Suitably educated and prepared, women should be able to control the work of delivery, so that it would be a natural function, with a good deal less pain and freed from the old ancestral fear. This approach created enormous interest at the time; it was highly popular and widely used, and apparently still is. As for the involvement of the planetary effect at birth, this can only work to the benefit of natural childbirth: labour is facilitated; the uterine contractions, which we now know to be partly stimulated by the foetus, are more effective; and the intervention of the doctor becomes less often necessary, reducing in particular the frequency of forceps deliveries caused by excessively long labour.

However, this most welcome psychological revolution has been followed by a technological revolution opposed to natural laws. Chronobiologists (those who study rhythms) have found that it is much better not to meddle with the biological clock of the child and to let it be born according to its natural rhythm, that is, at night or in the early hours of the morning.[5] But, for the doctor's convenience, the child is now compelled to be born in the daytime. It is very sad, as well as paradoxical, that doctors today recognize the positive role played by the foetus during delivery, yet interfere with the body of the mother by giving drugs to induce labour. Natural childbirth has helped the mother to feel like a human being, playing an active part in her child's entry into the world. But doctors are now reducing the mother to a passive object in the hands of an omnipresent technology, with its battery of surgical, electronic and medical resources. What happens to the subtle machinery linking foetus and planet in all this? My experiments provide the answer: it seizes up slightly, a lot, completely, depending on the potency of the medicine.

Of course, doctors have not acted from purely selfish motives, but have been trying to improve labour in a therapeutic way. Little progress was made before the beginning of this century, and they proceeded cautiously after the First World War, then on a larger scale after the Second, until what had been pioneering experiments on isolated cases became common practice, and the techniques themselves highly sophisticated. This is the technological revolution, which I shall now examine.

Amniotomy, or the artificial rupture of the membranes, is a very old method. In the USA, the first such intervention was carried out in 1810 by Thomas C. James, professor of obstetrics at the University of Pennsylvania in Philadelphia. By 1938, N. J. Eastman could comment: 'The frequency with which labor is induced by artificial rupture of the membranes constitutes a notable trend in modern obstetrics.'[6] In France before the Second World War, amniotomy was practised quite routinely in several maternity hospitals, often, incidentally, when labour had already begun.

In 1972, the senior nurse of the maternity department at the hospital in Bourges, central France, told me that they had used this method for years. Its timing depended on the nurses' work rota: rather than performing the operation at the end of her shift, a nurse would prefer to wait for her replacement on duty, who would come fresher to the task and could observe the labour.

Rupturing the membranes is a mechanical process, and no drug is administered to the mother. It is agreed that the technique shortens labour by about one or two hours if carried out after the pains have already started. It does not really change the daily rhythm of births. But what happens to the planetary effect? Research on births in the Baudelocque maternity hospital in Paris, where amniotomy was commonly employed between 1923 and 1930, provides a rough answer. The planetary effect on heredity remains visible, but appears to produce itself slightly earlier in the children than in the parents. For instance, if the parents were born with Mars in the key sectors of rise or culmination, their child will have a tendency to be born with Mars slightly before those key sectors. There is no longer perfect synchronization between the parents' generation and their child's. The frequent practice of rupturing the membranes during labour seems to be the best explanation of this dislocation in the timing of the planetary effect (see figure 26).[7]

The use of forceps is another form of intervention in the birth process with a long history. It is designed to assist the emergence of the baby's head from the mother's womb, in the case of difficult deliveries, but in some countries has become a standard way of speeding up the final stages of labour. This happened occasionally in France before the Second World War, while in the USA forceps were very popular until chemical processes were developed. According to Danaë Brook, forceps deliveries accounted for some 65 per cent of births around 1960 in the USA.[8]

After consulting medical files, I observed that the planetary effect between parent and child lost its force when forceps were used. Planetary synchronization between births of parents and children in key sectors was even less clearly marked than in the case of artificial rupture of the membranes. Although the planetary effect on heredity did not completely disappear, it was drastically reduced in the children (see figure 27).

Labour is painful, so what could be more natural than to seek to diminish the pain? The growth of pharmacotherapy has led to

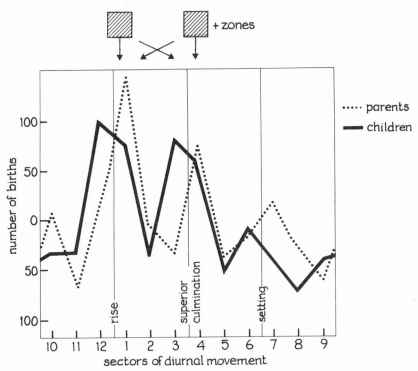

Figure 26 Amniotomy and dislocation of the planetary effect on heredity, with frequencies of the five significant planets added (see note 7)
Source: M. Gauquelin, series D, vol. II (1977)

a flood of analgesic products, intended to reduce the pain of childbirth, which today is a flourishing industry.

The appearance of pain-killers meant the introduction of chemicals into the blood of the mother and, consequently, that of the child, and interference with the subtle hormonal mechanisms of birth. The distant ancestor of these analgesics is chloroform, used for the first time when it was given to Queen Victoria in 1853 by John Snow, at the birth of Prince Leopold. There is, in fact, a whole battery of 'relaxing drugs', which are administered to the mother to make the uterine contractions more regular and labour more effective, but are not necessarily very powerful. 'Spasmalgine', for example, was widely used in France some forty years ago.[9]

In my study of births at the Créteil hospital near Paris, I noticed that Spasmalgine was administered fairly systematically

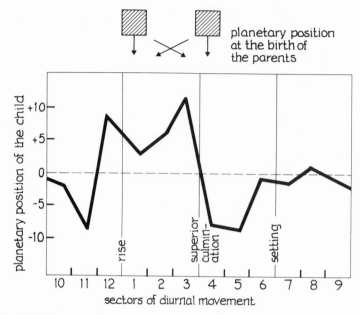

Figure 27 Forceps deliveries and dislocation of the planetary effect on heredity, with frequencies of the five significant planets added
Source: As figure 26

to mothers arriving at the hospital, when labour was already in progress, from 1938 onwards. I decided to compare the planetary effect on heredity in children born at Créteil before and after 1938, in other words without and with Spasmalgine. Again, the planetary effect shifted forward for those births where Spasmalgine had been used after 1938 (see figure 28). As the drug shortens the average length of labour, it seems highly likely that it causes this 'advance' in the planetary effect.

Spasmalgine, however, is a fairly mild, relaxing drug, and much stronger pain-killers are now available. According to Danaë Brook, these were used in 80 to 90 per cent of births in England as early as the 1970s.[10] One can imagine how much they must alter the planetary effect or even extinguish it.

But obstetrical medicine, confident in itself and its achievement, has not stopped there: the mechanization of childbirth has arrived, beginning with accelerated delivery, followed by the induction of labour, then monitoring and, finally, Caesareans for convenience.

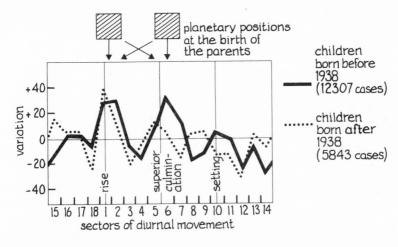

Figure 28   Children born before and after 1938 and dislocation of the planetary effect on heredity, with frequency reduced to the same scale and frequencies of the five significant planets added
Source: M. Gauquelin, *L'Hérédité Planétaire* (1966), p. 113

Stimulation of labour consists of controlling and increasing the rate of labour when it is already in progress in order to provoke uterine contractions. By the mid-1960s, according to two specialists, 'As uterine stimulants have been perfected and their modes of administration developed, their use has increased progressively. In modern obstetrics, some forms of stimulation may be utilized in as many as 20 per cent of labouring patients (in the USA).[11] The most common method is intravenous injection of a dilute solution of oxytocin, which is extremely efficient in activating contraction of the uterine muscle. But, with the administration of this or any similar drug, the role of the foetus is obscured and it loses control over the timing of delivery. The hormonal function is overwhelmed by the introduction of the drug into the mother's bloodstream at a high dosage and throughout the whole labour process.

The next stage in mechanization, elective induction of labour, is described by a specialist as follows: 'When complications of pregnancy are not present, an induction of labour is considered *elective*. The reasons for elective induction reveal an underlying philosophy relating to medical, obstetric, social and psychiatric advantages. Many of the elective inductions performed in the

United States would be classified as indicated inductions in other countries. . . . Elective inductions are considered unjustified by many authorities. They raise the possibility of increased risk with little benefit derived from such a procedure.'[12] Despite these reservations and as early as 1961, 'Elective induction of labour is well on its way to becoming an established part of American obstetrics. As more successful reports appear in the literature, its justification will become more widely accepted.'[13]

With the synthetic production of oxytocin and the appearance of postglandins – the two 'bestsellers' in the elective induction of labour – the era of childbirth by appointment has come about. Children can be born within office hours and outside weekends: not only the normal hour of birth has been changed, but the actual day. In an investigation of births in France and England between 1945 and 1978, Gérard Calot, director of the Institut National d'Etudes Démographiques, concludes:

> A study of the weekly profile of births and its changes over the last 30 years provides an example of the increasingly clearly marked effect of the intervention of man in a biological process. While, in the absence of medical intervention, the profile is visibly flat with a very slightly higher frequency on Sundays and Mondays, one can see in actual fact a minimum on Sundays, which gets lower and lower with every passing year. In England, the supreme country of the weekend, the phenomenon extends to a lesser degree to Saturday, and reaches even greater dimensions than in France: there are almost a quarter fewer births on a Sunday than on an average day in the year. . . . The medicalization of childbirth, now carried out exclusively in a hospital environment and more and more often induced artificially, is the basis for this increasingly clearly marked differentiation between the days of the week.[14]

Calot notes that the widespread practice of childbirth in a hospital environment allowed for a 'midwives' truce' over the Christmas period, though they compensated with increased activity from 27 to 29 December.

The process of 'monitoring' is another rung up the technological ladder. Here, the doctor does not simply decide when to trigger labour, but 'controls' it from beginning to end. A carefully estimated dosage of oxytocin is administered drop by drop into the mother's blood stream, and everything is standardized by means of the latest electronic equipment. In effect, it is child-birth by computer, a far cry from psychoprophylaxis and the mother's active participation in delivery. The procedure in 'machine-controlled labour' is outlined by Danaë Brook:

This baby machine manages to combine just about everything needed for an artificial labour. The woman has a strap round her stomach attached to a machine, which then automatically induces, monitors, controls and helps to deliver the baby by dilating the cervix. The induction agents used in computer-controlled labour are oxytocin and postglandins. Both, it is now known, cause a rise of bile pigment level in the baby's blood. The machine can also 'administer' Pethidine as a pain-killer. If contractions become unbearably strong because of the induction, it will then regulate their intensity by altering the rate at which the stimulating hor-mone is dripped to the mother intravenously. The contractions are monitored by way of a catheter threaded into the vagina, through the birth canal and inserted into the neck of the womb. The woman must stay on the machine for at least 30 minutes after delivery, as the strong inducing hormones increase the risk of maternal haemorrhage.[15]

Finally, there are Caesareans for convenience – by which I do not mean those operations which are necessary to protect the mother and save the child, but the ones performed just for the sake of greater 'comfort'. The mother must, of course, be anaes-thetized, either with a peridural, applying to only the lower part of the body, or with a general anaesthetic. In this way, the natural function of childbirth is transformed into a veritable surgical operation.

Professor Claude Sureau, head of the Baudelocque maternity hospital in Paris, gives the obstetrician's point of view: 'At the beginning, I was hesitant about opening the stomachs of these pregnant women but, literally pressured from one side by my patients and from the other by the anaesthetists, (I did so) and, I must say, if the mother demands it, I don't see any reason to refuse.[16] One wonders why a mother should voluntarily request a Caesarean, unless someone like a doctor had extolled its merits to her. Moreover, Professor Sureau does not refer to 'the preg-nant woman' or the 'mother-to-be' but the 'patient' – somebody ill, in effect. As Macfarlane comments, 'Mothers now having babies are considered "patients in hospital" rather than human beings going through normal physiological developments.'[17]

Some statistics will give an idea of the extent of the mechanization of childbirth. As early as 1975, 15 per cent of births in the Munich area in West Germany were Caesareans for convenience; the equivalent figure in England was about 10 per cent, although the proportion of induced labours reached 40 per cent in the same year.[18] France lags behind a little, but is fast becoming 'organized'. And the situation in the USA is portrayed by *Time* magazine, in a 1978 article:

> A decade ago, just one out of 20 babies born in the US was, in Shakespeare's phrase, 'from his mother's womb untimely ripp'd'. Doctors performed Caesareans only in cases in which normal delivery was impossible or the patient refused to endure vaginal delivery. Now there has been a sharp upswing in the number of Caesarians. Last year, at least one out of every ten babies in the US was delivered surgically. At major medical centers, which tend to handle more problem pregnancies, the share is even higher. The University Hospital of Cleveland at present deliver 12 per cent of all babies by C-sections (as Caesarean is called in hospital corridors). At the New York Hospital Cornell Medical Center, the figure is 22 per cent.[19]

Will all babies be born by Caesarean in a few years time? Or will something better have been worked out by then? Test-tube babies are already a reality, and soon perhaps the baby incubator, envisaged by Aldous Huxley in *Brave New World*, will be perfected and offered as an option to faint-hearted mothers. Doctors of the future – the not so distant future – can always justify themselves by saying, 'If the mother demands it, we cannot see any reason to refuse'.

But to return to the present, and to the planetary effect on heredity which, as might be imagined, has little scope under this heavy artillery of obstetrics. Although I have not yet researched into Caesareans for convenience, I have a record of several hundred cases where Caesarean delivery was considered necessary. The results produced by these are unsurprising and unambiguous: when children are born by Caesarean, the planetary effect on heredity disappears entirely (see figure 29).[20]

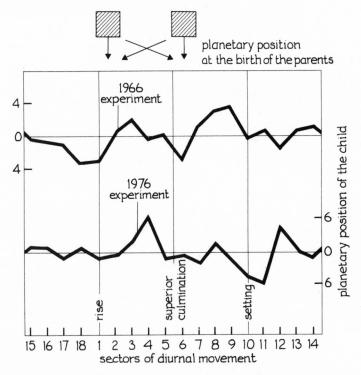

Figure 29 Children born with surgical intervention and the disappearance of the planetary effect on heredity, with frequencies of the five significant planets added
Source: M. and F. Gauquelin, *Replication of the Planetary Effect in Heredity,* series D, vol. II (1979)

One might ask whether those obstetricians who promote the mechanization of childbirth are forgetting their Hippocratic oath. Indeed, there is alarm in certain quarters, and even members of the medical profession have accused their colleagues of being swayed by fashion, of considering only their own comfort and of simply wanting to make more money. In 1981, *Science News* noted that 'Caesarean births increased by 300 per cent the past decade.' The article continues: 'Helen I. Marieskind, a Seattle health administrator, had done a study on the rising Caesarean rates for the Department of Health, Education and Welfare. . . . Some explanations emerged from her study as well – for instance, obstetricians performing C-sections to avoid mothers suing them for delivery of less-than-perfect babies (yet

health insurance data reveal that more malpractice claims are
filed for C-sections than for failure to perform C-sections);
obstetricians doing C-sections rather than vaginal deliveries
because the former earn more money.'[21]

And Danaë Brook writes: 'Having been introduced for very
good reasons, induction for social convenience is now being
encouraged by some gynaecologists, and a number of hospitals
have tried to bring in a policy of nine-to-five deliveries because
they fear that shortage of night staff might endanger the night-
born babies. However, according to the English medical paper,
the *Lancet*, there is some evidence to suggest that babies born
during the day might be more "vulnerable to the kind of distress
that requires oxygen administration".'[22] In fact, 'nine-to-five
deliveries' were already practised before the Second World War.
One pioneer was Professor de Forest, in New York. As he
describes it, towards the end of their pregnancy, women would
have a morning appointment booked at his office; at about nine
o'clock, labour was artificially induced and 'usually around the
middle of the afternoon, it reached the moment of expulsion and
before dinner time the child was born. . . . I ended by making
this routine practice my "standard" procedure.'[23]

A whole movement has grown up to counter obstetrical technology and return to 'ecological' childbirth. Its members are the
same people who fight against pollution, synthetic food and the
abuse of medicines, and they believe that obstetricians are contradicting nature. It is not that they want to revive the bad old
days of a hundred years ago, when deaths among newborn children were so high: all the developments in surgery, asepsis and
pharmacology should be available during the delivery, just as in
any other medical action. But when there is no need to intervene, nature should be allowed to follow her course.

The birth of a human being is much more than a simple
biological process, as R. D. Laing has observed:

To be born is a momentous event in our life cycle. In recent
years, hundreds of thousands of people have been going through
experiences as adults which they themselves feel to be related to
their actual birth experience. Traces of the experience of being

born seem to occur in dreams, myths, fantasies, physical events, or to be acted out in different ways. The preference for unnatural childbirth practices, which seems to be spreading across the world, despite countermovements to tune into the natural process, has led birth, in many places, to be a major psychobiological disaster zone, in which almost everything is done the exact opposite way from how it would happen, if allowed to.[24]

A birth is also a message of love, a promise of happiness. This is the fundamental assumption underlying the work of the French doctor, Frederick Leboyer – a belief which can be traced back, incidentally, to Paracelsus, the famous doctor and astrologer of the early Renaissance. Not content to criticize the loss of natural characteristics in childbirth Leboyer objects to the lack of consideration for the newborn child itself. He advocates a dark, quiet environment for the birth and bathing the child in water as soon as it is born, in order to make the transition from the mother's womb to the fresh air as gentle as possible. Leboyer writes: 'That instant of birth, with what respect it should be treated! What a fragile, fleeting moment it is. The child is between two worlds. At a gateway. He hesitates. Don't push him, don't hurry him! Let him take his time. Let this little being in. Let him do it in his own way, making the change from foetus to newborn child. . . . It is true that each child arrives with his own personality. . . . In spite of everything, birth is only an instant. To be sure. But a privileged instant.'[25]

Others have voiced their disapproval, more violently. Thus, Dr Michel Odent states: 'Obstetricians are technophrenes, that is, people who systematically empty their medical activity of all emotional content. . . . The history of obstetrics is the history of useless and dangerous manoeuvres invented to "favour" delivery.'[26]

A campaign has also been mounted for a revival of home delivery to stem the tide of technology. Defenders of modern childbirth techniques protest that this involves the mother and child in unnecessary risk, far from a well-equipped hospital theatre in the event of difficulties. Statistics, however, hardly justify the claim and, as Macfarlane points out, 'In all discussion of home versus hospital delivery, the childbirth practices in the Netherlands inevitably come up. Holland has a lower death rate among babies than either the United States or England, and yet a very substantial number of the deliveries are carried out at home.'[27]

G. L. Kloosterman, professor of obstetrics at the University of Amsterdam, has expressed thinking behind obstetric practice in the Netherlands since the beginning of the century: 'Childbirth in itself is a natural phenomenon and in the large majority of cases needs no interference whatsoever – only close observation, moral support and protection against human meddling. A healthy woman who delivers spontaneously performs a job that cannot be improved upon.'[28] In 1973, some 200,000 children were born in the Netherlands, half of them at home. The percentage of mortality among those born at home was three times lower than the percentage recorded for the Netherlands as a whole.

Obstetric policy is very different in Great Britain and the United States (in California, it is even against the law to have a home delivery.) 'It operates on the basis that it is impossible to predict which women will be "at risk", so that all women having babies must be treated as if they were high risk and hospitals are the places to deal with them. There is therefore an implicit "blackmail".'[29] Nevertheless, the efforts of 'childbirth ecologists' may be bearing fruit. In Great Britain, a very slight lowering of the percentage of induced births and C-sections was observable in 1977 and 1978 in comparison with the three earlier years.

Perhaps, in the end, the mechanization of childbirth will be only a passing fad, just as the custom of systematically removing children's tonsils and often their appendices (as a preventive measure) has now been reversed. But one may well fear that the robotization of childbirth is irreversible and that obstetricians and midwives will increasingly avoid working at night. For countries which have been scientifically less advanced, in South America, for instance, the discovery of obstetric technocracy is a marvel; they use it and abuse it.

For us today, it is a social phenomenon. Doctors have gradually persuaded women, through a skilful use of propaganda, not only to accept but also to demand induced births and Caesareans for convenience. Future mothers are led to believe that they will give their babies a better chance of life; they think of themselves too, and of the pain of childbirth. Macfarlane remarks:

> It is extremely interesting to compare the rate of use in different countries. According to a recent survey, drugs are given for pain in only 5 per cent of deliveries in Holland and in 12 per cent of deliveries in Sweden. Equivalent drugs are given in more than 80 per cent of deliveries in England. English women are not particularly noted to be any less stoical than their European counterparts – but why is there this huge difference? Is it because English doctors and midwives feel that drugs should be given routinely? Or could it be that Dutch and Swedish women know childbirth is going to be painful but accept pain as part of the whole process, whereas English women have been conditioned to believe that all pain must be relieved?[30]

British astrologers have started a 'campaign for birth times registration: putting pressure on Parliament to have the time of birth recorded on the birth certificate in England, Northern Ireland and Wales, as it already is in Scotland, is now official Astrological Association policy.'[31] Although I applaud their efforts, I can't help wondering how useful such precision would be if the hour of birth is to lose all significance through modern obstetrics. The moment of *natural* birth is a precious indicator of the hereditary temperament, and those who are aware of the fact must try to preserve intact this link binding us to the cosmos and the evolution of our species. It may be even more important than we think to safeguard natural births, for we are still totally ignorant of the exact influences of the planets at birth. To violate the laws of nature may have serious unknown consequences for the future and our descendants. The sociologists' phrase, 'the generation gap', is common parlance now, but that gap has never been so wide as it is today. It may not be too far-fetched to include, among its causes, the fact that some children are no longer born under the same planet as their parents. Convincing the scientific community of the reality of 'neo-astrology' is a question of patience. But we need time, and it may be that we do not have time.

But is the future of 'neo-astrology' as gloomy as that? As the reader will have realized, I feel very strongly about natural childbirth and have done for over 20 years, because it lies at the very heart of 'neo-astrology'. Indeed, the first French study to show the change from a natural rhythm of hours of birth through the day to a 'medical' rhythm appeared as early as 1959, and above Françoise Gauquelin's signature.[32] And it is many years since I pointed out the danger of neo-astrological statistics on births after 1950 becoming progressively meaningless. Later, in 1973, I was still without illusions but could show a qualified optimism: 'Perhaps one day we will be able to diagnose the planetary type to which an individual belongs from knowing his biochemical make-up. Then it will not be necessary to know the person's time of birth or the planetary configuration at the time of his birth. The diagnosis of astronomical temperament would become a biochemical matter. But as long as man and the solar system stay as they have been for thousands of years, the time of natural birth will always be, at least potentially, a valuable indication of a child's temperament.'[33]

Whatever the fate of natural childbirth, there remains one hope – that I have made a mistake about the facts. In other words, perhaps traditional astrology is right after all, and the sky at a 'medical' birth presents as much interest for neo-astrological science as the 'natural' birth sky.

In fact, we cannot judge whether a 'medical' sky is entirely without neo-astrological significance until there has been a sufficient lapse of time. My reasoning has been based on the disappearance of the planetary effect on heredity, as a result of which I concluded that it was useless to make any diagnosis of planetary temperament in the case of non-natural births. But, although the argument may seem unassailable, we need to wait until these children have grown to adulthood to be absolutely sure. It will then be possible to study their professional success and psychological personality, my other two experimental sources.

We may not have to wait that long. Sports champions represent the professional category in which, by definition, you have to be young to succeed. I already have a sample of some 200 well-known champions born after 1950, at a time when medicine was beginning to intervene in deliveries. In this case, it can be observed that the distribution of birth hours peaks around midday, instead of in the early hours of the morning, confirming that nature was not always left to her own devices.[34]

Moreover, the Mars effect in sports champions born after

1950 tends to disappear, just as I had suspected. Of course, the sample is too small to be entirely convincing on its own, and the absence of effect could be simply a matter of chance. These champions are young now, a familiar part of the present scene; but, in a few years, most will be completely forgotten, and it may turn out that some did not deserve their title of outstanding champions in the first place. Maybe, too, the modern approach to sport has something to do with the lack of the Mars effect: the systematic search for talent, the propaganda about titles and performances, the increasing importance of the coach (especially in American football)[35] – all these factors could explain why the new generation of sports champions does not necessarily show the Mars temperament, which their elders needed if they were to reach the top through their own efforts.

Of all these theories, only an experiment can tell which is right, and I intend to undertake one. It will entail, quite simply, listing the character traits of the new generation of champions to see whether these accord with the planet which was rising or culminating at their births. If the results are mediocre or poor, it will mean that planetary types can no longer be observed, or only with difficulty, in relation to the recent births of these sportsmen. One would then have to admit that the heavens, by becoming 'medicalized', are losing their diagnostic interest – which would be hard on astrologers, and on me.

But such an experiment would not prove the case conclusively so long as one did not take into consideration births which took place between 1950 and 1960. There were still a fair number of natural births then. We will have a clearer idea when we are able to experiment on character traits of people born after 1960 or, better, after 1970 or, better still, after 1980, since the percentage of medical births has increased dramatically recently. By the early years of the twenty-first century, we should know definitely what to believe. For the astrologers of that time, the year 2001 may be a very sad 'space odyssey' indeed. Perhaps I shall still be around to savour the bitter pleasure of being proved right, although there is still hope that I could be wrong which, in a way, I would prefer.

Between now and then, and well before, I trust there will be plenty to do. There is no reason why the delivery room should not be transformed into a field for experiments, as long as they are entirely safe, particularly when mother and baby have already become the luxury guinea-pigs of modern obstetrical medicine. So far, I have been content to observe while gathering birth data: now I would like to experiment actively, controlling the phenomenon and introducing variations into parameters during childbirth (the amount of hormone produced during labour in foetuses with a 'selected' planetary heredity; the use of a machine able to produce variable magnetic fields, and soon).

My work, which began with the 'astrological' notion of the birth hour, may find its eventual fulfilment in a biochemical formula to replace the information provided by the natal position of the major planets. Such a discovery would explain the sensitivity of the foetus to the cosmos at the time of birth, in function of its heredity. In order to get that far – if my hypothesis is correct – 'neo-astrology' must break out of the scientific ghetto and gain standing in its own right with, in practical terms, qualified personnel and access to maternity hospitals and laboratories. Otherwise, the development of understanding will remain very slow.

'Neo-astrology' is a frightening idea. Relatively speaking, it hardly matters whether a practical application of the planetary effect could be worked out in the future. What is really important is that these effects do exist, and my scientific opponents know that they do. That some Chaldean priest could have had the notion, however crude, that the child at birth and the planets are 'in sympathy'; that he could have glimpsed this true, yet 'absurd', idea without the aid of statistics or a telescope; that he could have attributed aggressiveness and warfare to Mars with none of the tools of modern knowledge – all this defies belief.

Scientists know that proof of planetary effects at birth would be equivalent in astrology to the Copernican revolution in astronomy. By claiming that the earth was not the centre of the universe, the monk Copernicus did not change man's daily life in the slightest degree. Yet his contemporaries stopped at nothing, not even crime, to keep the earth at the centre of the universe, so crucial was it to their understanding of the universe and the destiny of man. Think of Darwin, too, and the ructions caused by *The Origin of Species*, still rumbling on today. But the belief that 'man is descended from the monkey', or alternatively that he was created by God in the Garden of Eden – neither has any impact on our daily life. Technological developments such as electricity, the motor car and television have made a far deeper impression on the practical level, and have never provoked such major intellectual outbursts.

Schliemann's discovery in 1873, against all logic, that the city of Troy had actually existed, was entirely without practical application. Nevertheless, it was highly significant for our understanding of antiquity and archaeology, and it showed that there was a reality hidden in the songs of Homer.

The observation of planetary effects at birth would be a discovery of that magnitude. It would demonstrate, too, that the age-old, good-for-nothing, fossilized astrology was not pure legend after all. And that is the source of opposition to my work – the fear that an 'astrological' Copernican revolution would destroy a particular vision of the universe and shatter belief in a scientific creed which has excluded 'neo-astrology', just as it ignored the intuition of the Chaldean priest.

Can there be a Conclusion?

Let us observe the subtle observation made by the great Greek philosopher, that the man who makes a mistake is doubly ignorant, because he does not know the proper answer, and because he does not know that he does not know. It is that second ignorance which is serious, because the certainty felt by the man who mistakes the proper answer is indistinguishable from the certainty felt by the man who knows and does not make a mistake.

This advice from the mathematician, Emile Borel, served as an epigraph to my first book and seems even more appropriate today. It sums up the whole content of astrology, which is a question of ignorance. Where the mystery of astral influence is concerned, we are all, whatever the level of our knowledge and understanding, seeking a truth which evades us. It is that which draws us on: the magic of the cosmos casts its spell on everyone.

I am afraid that reading this book will have disappointed many of those who turned to it in search of intellectual comfort. Here, astrology has always remained enigmatic and, to the perfectly proper question, 'Should one believe it?', I can only answer by rejecting both the unconditional opponents and the confirmed upholders. Of course, I am aware that I have presented in these pages an astrology 'à la Gauquelin', a neo-doctrine for my own personal use. That is because the truth, the whole truth and nothing but the truth, does not exist in astrology – not yet, anyway. This is the only thing I am pretty sure of. My ideas on astral influence have changed continually, swinging back and forth like a pendulum. I deserve the double reproach of excessive credulity and extreme scepticism. And it has not always been easy to sustain my ambiguous dialogue with astrology – 'that great lady, come from afar, and in whose place today there reigns a whore', in the words of the poet André Breton.

Though I am so full of my subject, so determined to defend it, so proud of my discoveries, I am still tormented by two feuding demons. The first is the fear of having been mistaken in asserting that astral influence is real; the second is the agonizing thought of all I have been unable to discover or explain. After 30 years of critical consideration of astrology, my passion for it has not diminished. But today I would not allow myself to draw drastic conclusions as I have sometimes done in the past. I will be content simply to have thrown a little light on this vast mystery which has occupied so many great minds over the centuries.

Notes

PRELUDE: ASTROLOGY JUDGED

1 'Objections to astrology, a statement by 192 leading scientists', *Humanist* 35, no. 5 (September/October 1975).

2 George O. Abell, 'One astronomer's views', *Humanist* (January/February 1976).

3 Bouché-Leclerq, *L'Astrologie Grecque*, Leroux (Paris, 1899).

4 C. G. Jung, 'The spiritual problem of modern man' in *The Collected Works of C. G. Jung, X, Civilisation in Transition*, translated by R. F. C. Hull, Routledge (London, 1970), pp. 86–7.

5 Bart J. Bok, 'A critical look at astrology', *Humanist* (September/October 1975).

6 Carl Sagan, 'Readers' forum', *Humanist* (January/February 1976).

7 Ron Westrum, 'Scientists as experts: observations on "objections to astrology"', *Zetetic* I, no. 1 (1976), pp. 34–5.

8 Jean-Baptiste Biot, 'Relation d'un voyage fait dans le département de l'Orne pour constater la realité d'un météore observé à l'Aigle le 26 Floréal An II', Baudoin (Paris, 1803).

9 Paul Feyerabend, *Science in a Free Society*, chapter 6, 'The strange case of astrology', Schocken Books (1978).

10 Paul Feyerabend, *Against Method*, New Left Books (London, 1975).

11 Paul Couderc, *L'Astrologie*, PUF (Paris, 1978), p. 67.

12 Jean-Claude Pecker, *Le Ciel*, chapter, 'Le ciel inflexible de l'astrologie', Hermann (Paris, 1972).

13 Johannes Kepler, *Tertius Interveniens*, cited in Arthur Koestler, *The Sleepwalkers*, Penguin (London, 1964), p. 247.

14 Gérard Simon, *Képler, Astronome, Astrologue*, Gallimard (Paris, 1979).

15 Marcello Truzzi, 'Astrology: a review symposium', *Zetetic Scholar*, nos 3 and 4 (1979), p. 72.

16 Karl R. Popper, *The Logic of Scientific Discovery*, Hutchinson (London, 1959).

17 Henry Parkinson, 'Popper's fallibilism', *ETC, A Review of General Semantics* 35, no. 1 (1978).

18 I must admit that, while I am entirely in agreement with the notion of 'falsifiability' created by Popper, it does not seem to me such a new idea as all that. In asking an author to make his theory verifiable, pre-Popper scientists were practising 'falsifiability' without knowing it.

19 Luigi Aurigemma, *Le Signe Zodiacal du Scorpion dans les Traditions Occidentales de l'Antiquité Gréco-Latine à la Renaissance*, Mouton (Paris-La Haye, 1976).

20 Thomas S. Kuhn, *The Structure of Scientific Revolutions*, University of Chicago Press (1962).

21 Bok, 'A critical look at astrology'.

22 Marc Lachièze-Rey, 'Ondes de gravitation: une mise en evidence indirecte', *La Recherche* 102 (1979), pp. 776–7.

23 René Taton, *Causalité et Accidents de la Découverte Scientifique*, Masson, (Paris, 1955), p. 119.

24 Isaac Asimov, *Asimov's Biographical Encyclopedia of Science and Technology*, Allen & Unwin (London, 1966), pp. 293–4.

CHAPTER I: THE PLANETS OF SUCCESS

1 Michel Gauquelin, *Dreams and Illusions of Astrology*, Glover & Blair (London, 1980).

2 *Index Biographique des Membres, des Associés, et des Correspondants de l'Académie de Médecine*, Masson (Paris, 1939).

3 Michel and Françoise Gauquelin, *Méthode pour Etudier le Repartition des Astres dans le Mouvement Diurne* (Paris, 1957).

4 N. Imbert, *Dictionnaire National des Contemporains*, vols I–III (Paris, 1936–39).

5 Michel Gauquelin, *L'Influence des Astres, Etude Critique et Experimentale*, Le Dauphin (Paris, 1955).

6 Michel Gauquelin, *Les Hommes et les Astres*, Denoël (Paris, 1960).

7 Michel and Françoise Gauquelin, *Birth and Planetary Data Gathered since* 1949, series A: Professional Notabilities, vols. I–VI, Laboratoire d'Etude des Relations entre Rythmes Cosmiques et Psychophysiologiques LERRCP (Paris, 1970–71).
8 Michel and Françoise Gauquelin, *Profession-Heredity*, Results of series A & B, LERRCP (Paris, 1972).
9 The probabilities of the frequencies observed in the 'key sectors' were usually lower than a thousand to one, sometimes one in a hundred thousand, and even, occasionally, one in a million (for the exact figures, see note 8 above).
10 Michel Gauquelin, *Report on American Data*, series, vol. X, LERRCP (Paris, 1982).

CHAPTER 2: ENTER HEREDITY

1 Arthur Koestler, *The Sleepwalkers*, Penguin (London, 1964).
2 Paul Choisnard, *La Loi d'Hérédité Astrale*, Chacornac (Paris, 1919).
3 Karl E. Krafft, *Traité d'Astrobiologie*, Legrand (Paris, 1939).
4 Michel Gauquelin, *L'Influence des Astres*, 1st part, Le Dauphin (Paris, 1955). Michel Gauquelin, 'L'hérédité astrale', *Les Cahiers Astrologiques* 98 (1962), pp. 135–43. Michel and Françoise Gauquelin, *Statistical Tests of Zodiacal Influences*, Book 1: Profession and Heredity, series D, vol. III, LERRCP (Paris, 1978).
5 Michel Gauquelin, *L'Hérédité Planétaire*, Denoël (Paris, 1966), pp. 92–3; and 'Genetic sensitivity to external factors during the daily cycle of the deliveries', *Journal of Interdisciplinary Cycle Research* 2, no. 2 (1971), pp. 227–32.
6 Françoise Gauquelin, L'heure de la naissance', *Population* 4 (1959), pp. 683–709.
7 Michel and Françoise Gauquelin, *Birth and Planetary Data Gathered since* 1949, series B: Hereditary Experiment, vols. I–VI, LERRCP (Paris, 1970–71).
8 Michel and Françoise Gauquelin, *Replication of the Planetary Effect in Heredity*, series D, vol. II, LERRCP (Paris, 1977).
9 Michel and Françoise Gauquelin, *Profession-Heredity*, Results of series A and B, LERRCP (Paris, 1972); Michel Gauquelin, *The Cosmic Clocks*, Paladin (1973) (reprinted 1980); Michel Gauquelin, *Cosmic Influences on Human Behaviour*, Futura (London, 1976).
10 Michel and Françoise Gauquelin, *Diurnal Position of Sun, Mercury, Uranus, Neptune, Pluto (Profession-Heredity)*, series D, vol. V, LERRCP (Paris, 1978).

CHAPTER 3: 50,000 CHARACTER TRAITS

1   Michel Gauquelin, 'Image caracterielle des qualités favorables à la réussite professionelle', *La Caractérologie* 11 (1970), pp. 49–63.

2   Michel Gauquelin in *Les Cahiers Astrologiques* 29, no. 121 (1966), p. 80.

3   Michel Gauquelin, 'Essai de mise en évidence et de description d'une composante temperamentale dans l'effet planétaire d'hérédité, *Relazioni del XVI° Convegno della Salute* (1969), pp. 221–31; Gauquelin, 'Planeten und Charakterzüge', *Zeitschrift für Parapsychologie und Grenzgebiete der Psychologie* 14, no. 1 (1972), pp. 12–36.

4   J. Cohen, *Personality Assessment*, Rand McNally (Chicago, 1969).

5   G. W. Allport and H. S. Odbert, 'Trait-names: a psycho-lexical study', *Psychological Monographs* 47 (1936).

6   J. P. Chaplin, *Dictionary of Psychology*, Dell (1968).

7   H. and A. English, *Dictionary of Psychological and Psychoanalytical Terms*, Davis McKay (New York, 1958).

8   Allport and Odbert in *Psychological Monographs* 47 (1936).

9   *Ibid.*

10 H. J. Eysenck, *The Structure of Human Personality*, Methuen (London, 1970); R. B. Cattell, *The Scientific Analysis of Personality*, Penguin, (London, 1965).

11 Michel and Françoise Gauquelin, *Birth and Planetary Data Gathered since 1949*, series A: Professional Notabilities, vols. I–VI, LERRCP (Paris, 1970–71).

12 P. Neuveglise, *France-Soir*, 2 September 1970.

13 Michel and Françoise Gauquelin, *Psychological Monographs*, series C, vol. II, The Mars Temperament and Sports Champions (1973); vol. III, The Saturn Temperament and Men of Science (1974); vol. IV, The Jupiter Temperament and Actors (1974); vol. V, The Moon Temperament and Writers (1977), LERRCP (Paris).

14 *Ibid.*

15 David Cohen, 'Stars and planets', *Human Behavior* 5, no. 11 (1976), pp. 56–62.

16 D. E. Super, *The Psychology of Careers, an Introduction to Vocational Development*, Harper (New York, 1957); Miroslav Vanek and Bryant J. Cratty, *Psychology and the Superior Athlete*, Macmillan (London, 1970); 'The cultural origins of scientists', *New Society*, 21 January 1982.

17 For details of these figures, see note 1 above.

18 M. and F. Gauquelin, *Psychological Monographs*, series C.

19 Michel Gauquelin, R.-M. Deloche and F. Tanon, 'Temperamental significance of the planetary effect in heredity, methodology and results', *Journal of Interdisciplinary Cycle Research* 6, no. 1 (1975), pp. 60–70.

20 Michel and Françoise Gauquelin, *The Planetary Factors in Personality, their Permanence through Four Professional Groups*, series D, vol. I, LERRCP (Paris, 1978).

21 Michel and Françoise Gauquelin, *The Venus Temperament, a Tentative Description*, series D, vol. IV, LERRCP (Paris, 1978).

22 Michel and Françoise Gauquelin, *Psychological Monographs*, series C, vol. VI, Book of Synthesis (to be published).

23 Michel Gauquelin, *Report on American Data*, series D, vol. X, LERRCP (Paris, 1982), and *The Gauquelin Book of American Charts*, Astro Computing Services (San Diego, 1982).

24 Michel Gauquelin, *Spheres of Destiny*, Corgi (London, 1981).

25 Michel Gauquelin, *Cosmic Influence on Human Behaviour*, Futura (London, 1976).

CHAPTER 4: PERSONALITY AND THE PLANETS

1 Karl Popper, *The Logic of Scientific Discovery*, Hutchinson (London, 1959).

2 R. B. Cattell, *Personality and Motivation Structure and Measurement*, World Books (New York, 1957); Hans J. Eysenck, *The Structure of Human Personality*, Methuen (London, 1970).

3 Hans J. Eysenck, 'Primaries or second-order factors. A critical consideration of Cattell's 16PF battery', *British Journal of Social and Clinical Psychology* 11 (1972), pp. 265–9.

4 Hans J. and Sybil B. G. Eysenck, *Psychoticism as a Dimension of Personality*, Hodder and Stoughton (London, 1976).

5 Hans J. Eysenck and S. Rachman, 'Dimension of personality' in *Personality Assessment*, Penguin (London, 1966), p. 349.

6 Hans J. Eysenck, 'Planets, stars and personality' *New Behaviour* (1975), pp. 246–9.

7 Michel Gauquelin, *Les Hommes et les Astres*, Denoël (Paris, 1960); *Cosmic Influences on Human Behaviour*, Futura (London, 1976).

8 Michel Gauquelin, Françoise Gauquelin and Sybil B. G. Eysenck, 'Personality and position of the planets at birth: an empirical study', *British Journal of Social and Clinical Psychology* 18 (1979), pp. 71–5.

9 *Ibid.*

10 Michel Gauquelin, Françoise Gauquelin and Sybil B. G. Eysenck, 'Eysenck's personality analysis and the position of planets at birth: a replication on American subjects', *Personality and Individual Differences* 2 (1981), pp. 346–50.

11 Michel Gauquelin, *Murderers and Psychotics*, series D, vol. IX, LERRCP (Paris, 1981).

12 *Ibid.*

13 *Ibid.*

14 Michel Gauquelin, *The Spheres of Destiny*, Corgi (London, 1981).

15 Michel Gauquelin, 'Planets, personality and ordinary people', *Correlation* 1, no. 2 (1981), pp. 4–14.

16 Michel Gauquelin, 'Effet possible de la position natale diurne de certaines planètes sur les réponses données à un questionnaire vocationnel', *Les Cahiers Astrologiques* 29, no. 121 (1966), pp. 73–81; E. K. Strong, *The Vocational Interest of Men and Women*, Stanford University Press (1943).

17 Gauquelin, *Cosmic Influences on Human Behaviour.*

18 Gauquelin in *Correlation* 1 (1981).

19 Hans J. Eysenck, 'A note on Gauquelin's suggestions for studying ordinary people', *Correlation* 2, no. 2 (1982).

20 Alan Smithers, 'A comparative study of personality in relation to date of birth in the northern and southern hemispheres', *Correlation* 1, no. 1, (1981), pp. 15–25.

21 R. B. Culver and P. A. Ianna, *The Gemini Syndrome*, Pachart (Tucson, Arizona, 1979).

22 K. Pawlik and L. Buse, 'Selbst-Attribuierung als differentielle-psychologische Moderatorvariable', *Zeitschrift für Sozialpsychologie* 10 (1977), pp. 54–69; Hans J. Eysenck and D. K. B. Nias, *Astrology; Science or Superstition?*, Temple Smith (London, 1982).

23 Pawlik and Buse in *Zeitschrift für Sozialpsychologie* 10 (1977).

24 Gauquelin in *Correlation* 1 (1981).

25 D. B. Bromley, *Personality Description in Ordinary Language*, John Wiley (London, 1977).

26 *Ibid.*

CHAPTER 5: 'SCIENCE' AND PROOF

1 Michel Gauquelin, *L'Influence des Astres, Etude Critique et Experimentale*, Le Dauphin (Paris, 1955).

2 Paul Couderc, *L'Astrologie*, PUF (Paris, 1951 edn).

3 Michel Gauquelin, *Les Hommes et les Astres*, Denoël (Paris, 1960).

4 Bart J. Bok, letter to Michel Gauquelin, 2 June 1960.

5 Sylvain Arend, letter to Michel Gauquelin, 3 January 1956.

6 Jean Porte, 'L'influence des astres et la statistique', *La Tour Saint Jacques* 4 (1956), pp. 86–105.

7 Jean Porte, preface to Michel and Françoise Gauquelin, *Méthode pour Etudier la Répartition des Astres dans le Mouvement Diurne* (Paris, 1956).

8 Jean Dath, letter to Michel Gauquelin, 28 January 1962.

9 Giorgio Piccardi, preface to Michel Gauquelin, *L'Hérédité Planétaire*, Denoël (Paris, 1966).

10 Frank A. Brown, foreword to Michel Gauquelin, *The Cosmic Clocks*, Henry Regnery (Chicago, 1967).

11 Michel Gauquelin, letter to Professor Koenigsfeld, 4 March 1967.

12 Remy Chauvin, 'L'affaire Gauquelin' in *Certaines Choses que je ne m'explique pas*, Retz (Paris, 1976).

13 Michel Gauquelin, 'Possible planetary effects at the time of birth of successful professionals: an experimental control', *Journal of Interdisciplinary Cycle Research* 3, no. 3/4 (1972), pp. 381–9.

14 Comité Belge pour l'Etude des Phénomenes Réputés Paranormaux (Para Committee): 'Considérationscritiques sur une recherche faite par M. M. Gauquelin dans le domaine des influences planétaires', *Nouvelles Brèves* 43 (1976), pp. 327–43.

15 Luc de Marré, 'Comments on research on the Mars effect by P. Curry', *Zetetic Scholar* 9 (1982).

16 Paul Couderc, letter of 18 March 1968, in appendix to Alec Mellor, *Catholiques d'aujourd'hui et Sciences Occultes*, Mame (Paris, 1968).

17 Paul Couderc, 'Le cas M. G.' in *L'Astrologie*, PUF (Paris, 1974 edn).

18 Paul Couderc, 'Le cas M. G.' in *L'Astrologie*, PUF (Paris, 1978 edn).

19 Porte in Gauquelin, *Méthode pour Etudier la Répartition des Astres dans le Mouvement Diurne* (Paris, 1956).

20 Hans J. Eysenck, 'Planets, stars and personality', *New Behaviour* (1975), pp. 246–9. See also: Eysenck and D. K. B. Nias, *Astrology, Science or Superstition?*, Temple Smith (London, 1982). In this remarkable work, the authors devote a chapter to 'the work of the Gauquelins' which is called a 'very convincing case'.

21 Jean François Le Ny, letter to Michel Gauquelin, 15 March 1976.

22 Michel Gauquelin, 'A possible Mars effect at the time of birth of superior athletes', *Proceedings of IV International Society of Sport Psychology* (Prague, 1977), pp. 178–82.

23 Lawrence J. Jerome, 'Astrology: magic or science?', *Humanist* 35, no. 5 (September/October 1975).

24 Marvin Zelen, 'Astrology and statistics, a challenge', *Humanist* 36, no. 1 (January/February 1976).

25 Michel and Françoise Gauquelin, 'The Zelen test of the Mars effect', *Humanist* (November/December 1977), pp. 30–35.

26 Marvin Zelen, Paul Kurtz and George Abell, 'Is there a Mars effect?', *Humanist* (November/December 1977), pp. 36–9.

27 *Ibid.*

28 Elisabeth L. Scott, letter to Zelen, Kurtz and Abell, 12 April 1978.

29 H. Krips, 'Astrology – fad, fiction or forecast?' *Erkenntnis* 14 (1979), p. 373.

30 Eric Tarkington, 'Gauquelin's travels (being an account of the adventures of Dr Michel Gauquelin while shipwrecked in the lands of his various "scientific" critics)', *Phenomena* 2, no. 2 (1978), pp. 18–21.

31 Malcolm Dean, *The Astrology Game*, chapter 11, 'We, the undersigned', Nelson Foster and Scott (Don Mills, Ontario, 1980). The first person to mention a 'cover-up' by CSICOP in the affair of the Mars effect was Malcolm Dean in his journal *Phenomena* (March/April 1978).

32 Gauquelin, *Les Hommes et les Astres*.

33 Paul Kurtz, Marvin Zelen and George Abell, 'Results of the US test of the "Mars effect" are negative', *The Skeptical Inquirer* (winter 1979–80), pp. 19–26.

34 Michel and Françoise Gauquelin, 'Star US sportsmen display the Mars effect', *Skeptical Inquirer* (winter 1979–80), pp. 31–40.

35 Michel Gauquelin, letter to Paul Kurtz, 10 November 1978.

36 Michel Gauquelin, *The Mars effect and sports champions: a new replication*, series D, vol. VI, LERRCP (Paris, 1979).

37 Kurtz, Zelen and Abell, 'Results of the US test on the "Mars effect" are negative'.

38 Michel Gauquelin, letter to Paul Kurtz, 27 July 1980.

39 Paul Kurtz, letter to Michel Gauquelin, 27 July 1981.

40 Dennis Rawlins, 'sTarbaby', *Fate* (October 1981), pp. 67–98. I imagine the Anglo-Saxon reader will have no difficulty in understanding the joke about 'sTarbaby'. Here, as Rawlins makes clear in his article, Paul Kurtz and CSICOP play the part of Br'er Rabbit, and Gauquelin's Mars effect represents the Tarbaby.

41 Dennis Rawlins, 'Memorandum on the relation of Mars' solar proximity to M. Gauquelin's Mars-sports results and claims', *Phenomena* 2, no. 3 (1978), p. 22.

42 G. O. Abell sent me a letter on 3 May 1980 (with a copy to Kurtz), saying that he had repeated the calculations on Mars

without finding any methodological errors on my part. This control was unfortunately never made part of any official pronouncement by CSICOP.

43 Rawlins in *Fate* (October 1981).

44 *Ibid.*

45 *Ibid.*

46 Michel Gauquelin, letter to Paul Kurtz, 10 November 1978.

47 Richard Kamman, 'The true disbelievers: Mars effect drives skeptics to irrationality', *Zetetic Scholar*, 10 (1982).

48 R. A. McConnell, letter, 11 September 1981; McConnell and T. K. Clark, 'Guardians of orthodoxy: the sponsors of the CSICOP', *Zetetic Scholar*, 10 (1982).

49 *Skeptical Inquirer* (winter 1981–82) – articles, statements and letters about the Mars effect controversy.

50 'Marcello Truzzi talks about the crusade against the paranormal: part 1 and 2', *Fate* (September 1979), pp. 70–6, (October 1979), pp. 87–94.

51 Patrick Curry, 'Research on the Mars effect', *Zetetic Scholar* 9 (1982).

52 Marcello Truzzi, 'Introduction to "research on the Mars effect"', *Zetetic Scholar* 9 (1982).

53 Curry in *Zetetic Scholar* 9 (1982).

54 Jean-Claude Pecker, letter to the editor 'On astrology and modern science', *Leonardo* 8 (1975), p. 89; 'L'Astrologie et la science', *La Recherche* (January 1983), pp. 118–28.

55 Jean-Claude Pecker, letter to Michel Gauquelin, 25 November 1975.

56 Michel Rouzé, 'Effet Mars: la néo-astrologie en échec', *Science et Vie* (March 1981), pp. 39–45.

57 Philippe Cousin, letter to Michel Gauquelin, 26 March 1981.

58 Michel Gauquelin, 'Protocole pour vérifier s'il existe oui ou non un effet Mars'. (April 1982).

59 Since I produced the typescript of this book, a definitive protocol experiment, accepted by the CFEPP and myself, has been published in the October 1982 issue of *Science et Vie* ('L'effet Mars est-il réel?'). This is the first positive step after an eighteen-month wait. But what next?

60 Thomas S. Kuhn, *The Structure of Scientific Revolution*, University of Chicago Press (1970).

61 Patrick Grim (ed.), *Philosophy of Science and the Occult* (section 1, Astrology), State University of New York Press (1982).

CHAPTER 6: THE TRIUMPH OF THE ASTROLOGICAL IDEA

1 Ptolemy, *Tetrabiblos*, edited and translated by F. E. Robbins, Harvard University Press (1956). Manilius, *The Five Books*, translated in London, 1697, republished by the American Federation of Astrologers in 1953.

2 Margaret E. Hone, *The Modern Text Book of Astrology*, Fowler (London, 1951).

3 *Ibid.*

4 *Ibid.*

5 Paul Choisnard, *Langage Astral*, Charcornac (Paris, 1920).

6 Ptolemy, *Tetrabiblos*.

7 Hone, *The Modern Textbook of Astrology*.

8 Paul Conderc, *L'Astrologie*, PUF (Paris, 1974), p. 56.

9 *New Webster Dictionary*, international edn (1969).

10 Ptolemy, *Tetrabiblos*.

11 Michel Gauquelin, *Cosmic Influence on Human Behaviour*, 4th interlude, Futura (London, 1976).

12 Johnstone Parr, *Tamburlane's Malady and Other Essays on Astrology in Elizabethan Drama*, University of Alabama Press (1953).

13 Gauquelin, *Cosmic Influence on Human Behaviour*.

14 *Ibid.*

15 Michel and Françoise Gauquelin, *Psychological Monographs*, series C, vols. II–V, LERRCP (Paris, 1973–77).

16 Jeff Mayo, *Teach Yourself Astrology*, Fowler (London, 1970).

17 Françoise Gauquelin, *The Psychology of the Planets*, Astro Computing Services (San Diego, 1982).

18 Michel Gauquelin, 'Planetary influences: an empirical study on the accuracy of "ancient" astrologers' keywords', *Correlation* 2, no. 2 (1982).

19 Françoise Gauquelin, *Traditional Symbolism in Astrology and the Character-Trait Method*, series D, vol. VII, LERRCP (Paris, 1980).

20 Michel and Françoise Gauquelin, *Diurnal Position of Sun, Mercury, Uranus, Neptune, Pluto (Profession-Heredity)*, series D, vol. V, LERRCP (Paris, 1978).

21 Françoise Gauquelin, *Traditional Symbolism in Astrology*.

CHAPTER 7: THE HOROSCOPE FALLS DOWN

1 Michel Gauquelin, *L'Influence des Astres, Etude Critique et Experimentale*, Le Dauphin (Paris, 1955); *Astrology and Science*,

Peter Davies (London, 1970); Michel and Françoise Gauquelin, *Statistical Tests on Zodiacal Influences*, Part I: Profession and Heredity, series D, vol. III, LERRCP (Paris, 1978).

2 Michel Gauquelin, *Zodiac and Character Traits*, series D, vol. VIII, LERRCP (Paris, 1981); Gauquelin, 'Zodiac and personality: an empirical study', *The Skeptical Inquirer* 6, no. 3, (spring 1982), pp. 57–65.

3 Jeff Mayo, *Teach Yourself Astrology*, Fowler (London, 1970).

4 Gauquelin, *Zodiac and Character Traits*; and in *The Skeptical Inquirer* 6 (1982).

5 Paul Choisnard, *Le Calcul des Probabilités Appliqués à l'Astrologie*, Charcornac (Paris, 1914).

6 Paul Choisnard, *Preuves et Bases de l'Astrologie Scientifique*, Charcornac (Paris, 1919).

7 Karl E. Krafft, *Traité d'Astrobiologie*, Legrand (Paris, 1939).

8 Gauquelin, *L'Influence des Astres*.

9 Choisnard, *Preuves et Bases de l'Astrologie Scientifique;* Michel Gauquelin, *Dreams and Illusions of Astrology*, Glover and Blair (London, 1980).

10 Jacques Sadoul, *L'Enigme du Zodiaque*, Denoël (Paris, 1971).

11 *Correlation* (edited by Simon T. Best), published by the Astrological Association, is the best example of these new journals devoted to research into astrology.

12 Geoffrey Dean and Arthur Mather, *Recent Advances in Natal Astrology: a Critical Review 1900–1976*, Para Research (1977).

13 'Scientific astrology? A review symposium', *Zetetic Scholar* 3, no. 4 (1979), pp. 71–120.

14 John Addey, *Harmonics in Astrology*, Cambridge Circle (1976). John Addey died on 27 March 1982; he is a great loss to the serious astrological community.

15 Nona Press, 'Suicide in New York', *Journal of the National Council of Geocosmic Research* 3 (1978).

16 Edmund Van Deusen, *Astrogenetics*, Doubleday (New York, 1976).

17 Michel Gauquelin, 'Review of Van Deusen's *Astrogenetics*', *The Skeptical Inquirer* (spring/summer 1978), pp. 118–28.

18 S. Ostrander and L. Schroeder, *Astrological Birth Control*, Prentice Hall (1972).

19 R. Kimball and W. H. Kautz, 'On the validity of Jonas' theory, unpublished (1974–77), quoted in Dean and Mather, *Recent Advances in Natal Astrology*.

20 Ivan W. Kelly and Don H. Sakloske, 'An alternative explanation

in science: the extroversion-introversion astrological effect', *The Skeptical Inquirer* (summer 1981), pp. 33–7; Hans J. Eysenck, 'The importance of methodology in astrological research', *Correlation* 1, no. 1 (1981), pp. 11–14.

21 Hans J. Eysenck and Sybil B. G. Eysenck, *Manual of the EPI (Eysenck Personality Inventory)* (University of London Press, 1963).

22 J. Mayo, O. White and H. J. Eysenck, 'An empirical study of the relation between astrological factors and personality', *Journal of Social Psychology* 105 (1978), pp. 229–36.

23 M. Jackson and M. S. Fiebert, 'Introversion-extroversion and astrology', *Journal of Psychology* 105 (1980), pp. 155–6; A. Veno and P. Pamment, 'Astrological factors and personality: a southern hemisphere replication', *Journal of Psychology* 101 (1979), pp. 73–7; D. H. Saklofske, I. W. Kelly and D. W. McKerracher, 'An empirical study of personality and astrological factors', *Journal of Psychology* 110 (1982), pp. 275–80.

24 K. Pawlik and L. Buse, 'Selbst-Attribuierung als differentielle-psychologische Moderatorvariable', *Zeitschrift für Sozialpsychologie* 10 (1979), pp. (1979), pp. 54–69.

25 H. Eysenck, in *Correlation* 1 (1981).

26 Z. Dobyns, 'Review of *Cosmic Influence on Human Behavior* by M. Gauquelin', *Psychology Today* (September 1974), p. 131.

27 R. B. Culver and P. A. Ianna, *The Gemini Syndrome*, Pachart (Tucson, Arizona, 1979).

28 Vernon Clark, 'Experimental astrology', *In Search* (winter and spring, 1961).

29 Jacques Sadoul, *L'Astrologie*, Retz (1972).

30 Paul Colombet, *Les Cahiers Astrologiques* (September/October 1961, May/June 1962).

31 Dal Lee, quoted in M. Gauquelin and J. Sadoul, *Les Trois Faces de l'Astrologie*, Retz (1972), p. 244.

32 J. E. Vidmar, 'Astrological discrimination between authentic and spurious birthdates', *Cosmology Bulletin* 8/9 (1979).

33 Michel Gauquelin, 'L'astrologue paré de l'IBM', *Science et Vie* 611 (August 1968), pp. 80–9, reprinted and translated in *The Aquarian Agent* (New York, 1971).

34 Gauquelin, *Dreams and Illusions of Astrology*, chapter 6, 'The sign of the computer'.

35 C. R. Snyder, 'Why horoscopes are true: the effects of specificity on acceptance of astrological interpretations', *Journal of Clinical Psychology* 30 (1974), pp. 577–80.

36 Ray Hyman, 'Cold readings: how to convince a stranger that you know all about them', *The Skeptical Inquirer* (spring/summer 1977).

37 *Ibid.*

38 Anthony Standen, *Forget Your Sun Sign*, Legacy (1977).

CHAPTER 8: 'MIDWIFE' PLANETS?

1 Michel Gauquelin, *L'Hérédité Planétaire*, Denoël (Paris, 1966), p. 121.

2 Aidan Macfarlane, *The Psychology of Childbirth*, Fontana, Open Books (1977).

3 Professor Robert Debré, *France-Soir*, 12 April 1975.

4 G. S. Dawes, 'Chairman's opening remarks', *Foetal Autonomy*, Ciba Foundation (1969).

5 Michel Gauquelin, 'Comment un enfant est nait et pourquoi au 9 ième mois', *Science et Vie* 68 (1970).

6 'The baby's role in timing birth', *Medical News Tribune* (25 October 1971).

7 Macfarlane, *The Psychology of Childbirth*.

8 Fritz Fuchs, statement to the journalist Zullo, December 1976.

9 Macfarlane, *The Psychology of Childbirth*.

10 *Ibid.*

11 J. D. Ratcliffe, *La Naissance*, Stock (Paris, 1953), p. 56.

12 Gauquelin, *L'Hérédité Planétaire*.

13 Michel Gauquelin, 'Note sur le rythme journalier du début des douleurs de l'accouchement', *Gynécologie et Obstétrique* 66, no. 2 (1967), pp. 229–36.

14 The labour of 'primiparous' (first baby) mothers lasts longer than that of 'multiparous' (subsequent babies) mothers. Nonetheless, I have observed no difference in planetary heredity between first and subsequent children. The zones of the sky where the planetary tendency dominates remain the same suggesting that, whatever the length of a natural delivery, the foetus comes into the world at the planetary time corresponding to its hereditary temperament. See notes 1 above and 29 below.

15 Lee Ratzan, 'The astrology of the delivery room', *Humanist* (November/December 1975).

16 George O. Abell, *Exploration of the Universe*, Holt, Rinehart and Winston (1973).

17 Ratzan in *Humanist* (November/December 1975).

18 R. B. Culver and P. A. Ianna, *The Gemini Syndrome*, Pachart
    (Tucson, Arizona, 1979).
19 *Ibid.*
20 *Ibid.*
21 Michel Gauquelin, 'L'effet planétaire d'hérédité en fonction de la
    distance de Vénus et de Mars à la terre', *Cahiers Astrologiques* 136
    (1968), pp. 561–9.
22 Paul Couderc, *L'Astrologie*, PUF (Paris 1974 edn), pp. 118–19.
23 *Ibid.*
24 Anthony Standen, *Forget Your Sun Sign*, Legacy (1977), p. 103.
25 F. A. Brown, J. W. Hastings and J. D. Palmer, *The Biological
    Clock*, Academic Press (New York, London, 1970); A. S. Pres-
    man, *Electromagnetic Fields and Life*, Plenum Press (New York,
    London, 1970).
26 Beverley E. Pearson Murphy, 'Does the human foetal adrenal
    play a role in parturition?' *American Journal of Obstetric Gynae-
    cology* (15 February 1973).
27 Julius Bartels, *Daily International Character C, from 1884 to 1961*
    (Göttingen, 1962).
28 Gauquelin, *L'Hérédité Planétaire*; Gauquelin, *Cosmic Influence on
    Human Behaviour*, chapter 17, Futura (London, 1976); Gauquel-
    in, 'A possible hereditary effect on time of birth in relation to the
    diurnal movement of the Moon and the nearest planets; its
    relationship with geomagnetic activity', *Proceedings of Fourth
    International Biometereological Congress, International Journal of
    Biometeorology* 11, Supplement (1967), p. 341.
29 Michel and Françoise Gauquelin, *Replication of the Planetary
    Effect in Heredity*, series D, vol. II, LERRCP (Paris, 1977).
30 Couderc, *L'Astrologie*.
31 I. Lakatos, *The Methodology of Scientific Research Programmes*,
    Cambridge University Press (London, 1978).

CHAPTER 9: 'NEO-ASTROLOGY' UNDER ATTACK

1 Aidan Macfarlane, *The Psychology of Childbirth*, Fontana, Open
   Books (1977).
2 Karl E. Krafft, *Traité d'Astrobiologie*, Legrand (Paris, 1939).
   Gérard Simon, *Kepler, Astronome, Astrologue*, Gallimard (Paris,
   1979).
3 Carl Gustav Jung, *Synchronicity, an Acausal Connecting Principle*,
   Routledge (London, 1955).

4 G. Dick-Read, *Childbirth without Fear*, Heinemann (London, 1968, first published 1933); Fernand Lamaze, *Painless Childbirth: Psychoprophylactic Method*, translated by L. R. Celestin *et al.*, Burke (London, 1958).

5 J. Malek, J. Gleich and V. Maly, 'Characteristics of the daily rhythm of menstruation and labor', *Annals of the New York Academy of Sciences* 98 (1962), p. 1042.

6 N. J. Eastman, *American Journal of Obstetric Gynaecology* 35 (1938), p. 721.

7 Michel and Françoise Gauquelin, *Replication of the Planetary Effect in Heredity*, series D, vol. II, LERRCP (Paris, 1977). An alternative explanation, which could be combined with amniotony, is episiotomy or surgical incision to enlarge the vaginal orifice (which is now, according to Danaë Brook, 'standard procedure in almost all hospital deliveries'). Episiotomy, like amniotomy, shortens the delivery.

8 Danaë Brook, *Naturebirth*, Penguin (London, 1976).

9 H. Vignes, *Les Douleurs de l'Accouchement*, Masson (Paris, 1951).

10 Brook, *Naturebirth*.

11 Harry Fields, John W. Greene and Kaighn Smith, *Induction of Labor* (Macmillan, 1965).

12 Macfarlane, *The Psychology of Childbirth*.

13 Fields, Greene and Smith, *Induction of Labour*.

14 Gérard Calot, 'Le mouvement journalier des naissances à l'intérieur de la semaine', *Population* 3 (1981), pp. 477–504.

15 Brook, *Naturebirth*.

16 Claude Sureau, 'Comment naître sans danger', *Parents* 118, (December 1978).

17 Macfarlane, *The Psychology of Childbirth*.

18 Calot in *Population* 3 (1981).

19 'Caesareans up', *Time*, 27 March 1978.

20 M. and F. Gauquelin, *Replication of the Planetary Effect in Heredity*; Michel Gauquelin, *Cosmic Influences on Human Behaviour*, chapter 16, Futura (London, 1976).

21 'More attacks on Caesarean deliveries', *Science News* (June 1981).

22 'A time to be born', *Lancet* (16 November 1974), p. 1181, cited in Brook, *Naturebirth*.

23 Gauquelin, *Cosmic Influences on Human Behaviour*; A. Klopper and J. Gardner (eds), *Endocrine Factors in Labour*, Cambridge University Press (London, 1973).

24 R. D. Laing, *The Facts of Life*, Penguin (London, 1977), p. 64.

25 Frederick Leboyer, *Birth without Violence*, Knopf (New York, 1975); also Wildwood House (London, 1975).

26 Michel Odent, *Bien Naître*, Le Seuil, (Paris, 1976).

27 Macfarlane, *The Psychology of Childbirth*.

28 G. J. Kloosterman, 'Obstetrics in the Netherlands: a survival challenge?', *50th Anniversary of the International Confederation of Midwives* (1972).

29 Macfarlane, *The Psychology of Childbirth*.

30 *Ibid.*

31 'Campaign for birth times registration', *Transit: The Astrological Association Newsletter* (January 1982).

32 Françoise Gauquelin, 'L' heure de la naissance', *Population* 4 (1959), p. 683.

33 Gauquelin, *Cosmic Influences on Human Behaviour*.

34 Michel Gauquelin, *The Mars Effect and the Sports Champions: A New Replication*, series D, vol. VI, LERRCP (Paris, 1979).

35 Bryant J. Cratty, *Psychology in Contemporary Sport, Guidelines for Coaches and Athletes*, Prentice Hall (1973).

Index

APPENDIX: A QUESTIONNAIRE

In one of my previous books I included a questionnaire which I hoped would help me in my research. Readers were asked to assess their own characters and send me the results, together with information about their birth. I found that people had difficulty in assessing themselves fairly, so in this questionnaire I have asked you to get someone else, or preferably two other people, to assess you as well. You may find it interesting to find out what other people really think of you!

Personal details

male/female ....

place of birth ....

date of birth ....

time of birth .... am/pm

source of time of birth information: birth certificate / family records / other (give details)...............................

....

....

delivery information: natural / Caesarean / induced / forceps
other factors which may have affected the precise timing of your birth

....

....

Character assessment

From the following list of 100 character traits please choose ten which you feel most accurately describe your personality, and ten which are least applicable to you. Then get someone else to do the same (without showing them your answers). The more people you ask to assess your character in this way the better.

1 well-dressed	2 eloquent	3 brilliant
4 enthusiastic	5 fearful	6 hardened
7 bold	8 tough	9 tenacious
10 scrupulous	11 argumentative	12 reserved
13 witty	14 sporty	15 passive
16 timid	17 immodest	18 courageous
19 punctual	20 capricious	21 indecisive
22 unfashionable	23 exuberant	24 dissipated
25 self-controlled	26 apprehensive	27 dreaming
28 not adventurous	29 unemotional	30 attentive
31 realistic	32 eager	33 lively
34 changeable	35 humorous	36 impulsive
37 reckless	38 adventurous	39 sociable
40 modest	41 sensitive	42 pompous
43 orderly	44 bombastic	45 quiet
46 composed	47 studious	48 discreet
49 harsh	50 unpretentious	51 minutely careful
52 relaxed	53 coarse	54 humorless
55 quarrelsome	56 self-assured	57 indefatigable
58 precise	59 scientific	60 snobbish

61 pretentious	62 harsh	63 enterprising
64 amusing	65 domineering	66 authoritarian
67 pessimistic	68 gentle	69 vain
70 sophisticated	71 nonconformist	72 spendthrift
73 undisciplined	74 fearless	75 intrepid
76 audacious	77 shrewd	78 cautious
79 obstinate	80 rash	81 inoffensive
82 methodical	83 nonchalant	84 boastful
85 talkative	86 driving	87 headstrong
88 conservative	89 aggressive	90 not sporty
91 theatrical	92 impressionable	93 opportunistic
94 energetic	95 verbose	96 conventional
97 self-satisfied	98 eccentric	99 austere
100 irresolute		

Self-assessment (to be filled in by you)

The numbers of the ten traits which I think best describe my personality are:

The numbers of the ten traits which I think least applicable to my personality are:

External assessment (to be filled in by someone else)

The numbers of the ten traits which I think best describe his/her personality are:

The numbers of the ten traits which I think least applicable to his/her personality are:

My relationship to the person assessed is that of: family member / close friend / colleague / other (please specify)

. . . .

Notes

1 Delivery information is extremely important for people under thirty (ask your parents if you don't know about this).
2 Please do list exactly ten traits in each category.
3 If possible, please get several people to assess you, and add their individual results on a separate sheet.
4 **Please send completed forms, anonymously if you prefer, to Michel Gauquelin, Director, LERRCP, 8 rue Amyot, 75005 Paris, France.**